4-49

CV's
& Written
Applications

Copyright © Templar Publishing Ltd 1987

First published in Great Britain in 1987
by Ward Lock Limited, Artillery House, Artillery Row,
London SW1P 1RT, a Cassell Company

Reprinted 1989 (twice)

The Publisher and copyright holder wish to point out that all names
and addresses used as examples within this book are fictitious, and
are not intended to represent existing companies or individuals.

Designed and produced by Templar Publishing Ltd
Pippbrook Mill, London Road, Dorking, Surrey RH4 1JE
Typeset by Templar Type

Printed and bound in Great Britain
by Richard Clay Ltd.

British Library Cataloguing in Publication Data

Skeats, Judy
    C V's and written applications
    1. Résumés (Employment)
    I. Title
    650.1'4   HF5383

ISBN 0-7063-6612-3

CV's
& Written
Applications

Judy Skeats

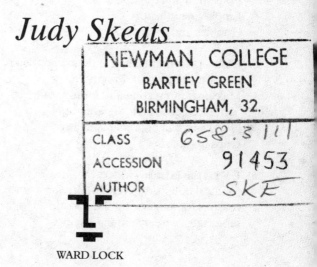

WARD LOCK

Contents

Acknowledgements

The author wishes to acknowledge the help of Serena Ringer and Mary McCullough for their practical hints and Nick Garlick for the wordprocessing helpline. Thanks to Sue, Anne, Tim, GB and my parents for all their support, too.

1. Introduction

The curriculum vitae is your passport to success. You must use it.

A carefully produced CV and application letter is the vehicle by which you sell yourself. It is generally your first contact with the employer and is an example of your work. If it makes no impact, particularly in situations where there are many applicants, it will be forgotten. No interview. And no job.

Even senior executives make many basic mistakes. CV's are not life histories or autobiographies. They should give factual information about the candidate without going into great detail of what the writer really wanted to be. They are designed to give a summary of salient factors about yourself. They must be brief and true and not turn into novels!

When drawing up your CV it is very important that you allow enough time to do this properly. How can you expect any organisation to employ you for a number of years if you cannot spare them enough time to think about what you are saying?

This book aims to help you to market yourself successfully. The following chapters take you through the art of understanding the advertisement and what is required, drawing up your CV, letters of introduction, finding out more about the company, how to angle your experience to fit the post and ways in which to beat the opposition.

This book assumes that you will be applying for jobs within the United Kingdom. If this is not the case, you must research the company even more thoroughly and fall in with the local customs. In some countries of the world, for instance, it is customary to tell the employer in what high esteem you hold him/her and that you want the post with all your heart! This would be seen as impossibly idiosyncratic in the UK.

Competitiveness in the labour market makes it possible for employers to be more discerning than ever before, so it is essential to have a good CV. The words you use and the layout you choose can be critical in making a good initial impression. Your aim is to give the reader an image of you as the candidate who can do the job. The CV, like the application form, must be geared towards the vacancy. This means that you must plan your approach, analyse the advertisement for implications as well as obvious requirements and write the application accordingly. There must be a logical progression from seeing the advertisement which interests you to the compilation of a curriculum vitae in which all the information is relevant to that job. If the application and CV is to be sent unsolicited to a company, it must be geared to that organisation and to the type of work you hope to gain.

Although the covering letter is valuable (and a chapter in this book is devoted to it), CV's must be able to stand alone as many firms will photocopy these and circulate them within the company to various selectors.

Most recruiters want to see a traditional CV and you must be seen as the 'safe' candidate. Recruiting is expensive and the employer must be convinced that you will stay in the company for a reasonable length of time, perhaps progressing within the firm. The employer does not want to recruit people who are too good for the job who will get bored and leave or disrupt the other employees.

It is vitally important that you allow yourself enough time in which to scrutinise the advertisement and compose an application which does you credit. The application must be thoroughly prepared. The preparation of CV's, application forms and covering letters all takes time if the process is to be effective. The application must fit the type of employment that you are seeking and the organisational culture. If you seriously want that position for your future career, it is not enough to write a letter, find an old CV from your filing cabinet and hope. All these things must be carefully planned. NEVER send your first draft without rechecking it or asking the advice of others first. You should not delay your response unnecessarily but neither should you rush it. This is your introduction to the company. Your job is to convince them that you can perform the tasks required, that you are interested in that company and that you merit an interview. Remember that in many cases the CV will influence the format and style of the interview because it will be based on information that you have given.

In many fields, the demands of the market place are constantly changing and you will therefore need to update and revise your CV regularly. You may also want to keep a long and a short version of your CV, for your own information and so that you will be able to provide more information for a particularly interested prospective employer.

Although this book is designed to be read straight through if necessary, so that the novice CV writer can take account of all the points before beginning, some points have been repeated in different chapters so that you will be able to turn directly to the relevant section and peruse that. In addition, there are appendices showing examples of good curriculum vitae and a list of points of contact and useful reading for those who still need more.

This book aims to deal with all aspects of writing CV's, filling in application forms and composing covering letters. It deliberately avoids all aspects of interviews and interview techniques. Many other publications have been produced which explore this area fully and some are listed in the section on further information. You may wish to read one or several such books in conjunction with this to refine your job search. Following the guidelines in this book should leave you at the door to the interview room, and pick you up again as you leave to deal with some helpful pointers for follow-up letters afterwards.

2. Understanding the advertisement

Understanding the advertisement is the key to the whole process. Your application and CV should be designed with the vacancy in mind, so it is vitally important that you are able to analyse the advertisement and make the correct deductions from it.

There are a number of aspects which personnel specialists have in mind when drawing up the copy for the advertisement. Constraints imposed by the organisation can also tell you a lot more. Consider the advertisement shown below.

SUPER COMPUTER SYSTEMS Ltd

... live and work in the beautiful countryside around Exeter

SALARIES UP TO £25,000

At our site just outside Exeter, which is engaged in the research and development of a range of computers and business systems for domestic use, we are seeking to increase our team with experienced and well qualified specialists in...

SOFTWARE DESIGN SYSTEMS ANALYSIS LASER SYSTEMS

Ideally, you'll have varied experience. However, we are also interested in hearing from individuals whose background includes display and graphics. If you have the right qualities and experience, salaries of up to £25,000 could be offered. The attractive benefits package also includes assistance with relocation costs.

If you are aged between 25 and 40, want to live in this delightful location, working for a rapidly expanding company, please ring David Coster on Exeter (0392) 123456, or write to Super Computer Systems Ltd., Exeter Road, Exeter, Devon EX1 1AA.

SUPER COMPUTERS – *Technology at its best*

This is typical of the advertisements found in the computing sections of quality newspapers and gives a large amount of information. The beginning of the advertisement tells the reader the name and location of the company in a positive way. It is well designed in terms of impact and shape. £25,000 catches the eye – the reader is usually already interested and reading further before noticing that this says 'up to'. The fact that the salary figure appears at the beginning is an indication, not only that the rates are very good, but also that the company knows that and pays good salaries in order to attract the right calibre of applicant. The relocation package reinforces that inference.

The advertisement says that the organisation is seeking a number of specialist staff, rather than just one post being vacant. The name of the person to reply to is clearly given, showing both a telephone number and address. David Coster has time to talk to applicants who ring and his office is well prepared for the onslaught of candidates.

These are just some of the points that you may notice immediately. Examples of the sorts of factors to look for are given below. Analysing advertisements takes time. You should check several factors, making notes on the information you have found. Once you have completed that, you will be in a position to start thinking about drafting your application letter and CV.

Job title

Notice how the post is described. This will give you an idea of how the company sees it. In the example given above more than one job is being advertised and the company has asked for specialists in each field instead of quoting the job titles. Where companies are advertising for secretaries, the title can mean many different things. The word 'secretary' may be misleading, describing either the work of a clerk/typist or an effective, high calibre personal assistant to a managing director of a multinational company. There may

11

be some narrative accompanying the title which will give you a clearer notion of exactly what the position entails.

Look at the wording of the advertisement to see if there is any indication of whether the successful applicant would work as part of a team, or mainly alone. This may be stated or seen to some extent from the level of supervision which is apparent.

Qualifications and experience

In some cases, the qualifications and experience needed will be clearly stated. In this case, the company has left it to the individuals to decide whether their own backgrounds would fit the requirements. Any expert in this field should know what is required for this kind of work and the sort of competition that he or she would face.

Salary and conditions

In many cases the actual salary to be offered is not quoted. Euphemisms such as 'attractive salary package', 'salary commensurate with age and experience' and 'right rewards for the right person' are employed. The golden rule is that if the salary is particularly attractive, it will be quoted, probably just beneath the job title where it can be used as a selling point. In our example of Super Computer Systems, the salary offered was good. It was also put into a prominent position and the reader could be nearly at the end of reading before the phrase 'up to' was noticed. The advertisement has succeeded in at least part of its function by persuading the reader to get that far. This is obviously vital in an industry where talent is scarce.

Look at what is said about the salary. The word 'circa' may mean 'around', but can be taken by the potential applicant as a minimum. The company is prepared to pay more than that, whilst not wanting to be as flexible as in the 'right salary for right person' advertisements. Quoting remuneration in terms of 'circa' also means that it does not waste the time of applicants and companies whose ideas are radically different.

Neither party wants to find itself at the interview stage before discovering that their expectations are entirely different.

Many advertisements, especially for posts in the public sector, give salary ranges. This shows interested applicants what their potential would be as well as the starting salary. Most organisations are able to raise the starting salary from the minimum if this is necessary to attract the right person, but it would be difficult to increase this by more than 10% unless you are a specialist. You must consider what you think your chances of being engaged on a rate above this would be.

In some advertisements, salary levels are not even mentioned. In those cases, you may safely assume that the salary package is fairly low – if it was very good, the organisation would not be shy about it! Attracting the best candidates may not come cheaply and recruiters are aware of this. There are exceptions to the rule though; for example, where there is never a shortage of applicants or where the company is determined to attract staff on the basis of interesting work rather than monetary rewards.

Other points to look for are whether the organisation concentrates on high commission levels (common in advertisements for sales people, but often means low basic pay). Alternatively, the benefits offered may add up to a good overall package rather than specifically high starting rates. The advertisements may attempt to interest the reader in future promotion prospects rather than immediate gains.

In all these examples, you must ask yourself why anyone searching for staff would word their sales pitch in such a way. You may find that all is explained by having a little knowledge of the organisation itself and the way in which it functions. (This is covered in a later chapter about how to find out more about your prospective employer.)

Location

In many cases, the location will be shown as the place to reply to. Sometimes, as in the example above, the recruiters make a virtue of this. Locations may be quoted at the top of advertisements (particularly where an agency is advertising) in terms of the town itself or the general area, eg. 'based in SouthWest England', or omitted entirely. The location of the job may be different from the reply address if the company's head office is advertising for one of its satellite sites.

In cases where the advertisement appears in local papers, there should be no real problem. It is a point to bear in mind though, that where the exact location is not given, the advertiser may realise that this is not a desirable place, may be ashamed of it or not want other employees to find out about impending relocation.

Company description and philosophy

Look at what the company says about itself. This tells you how it wants to perceive itself rather than how outsiders see it. This is important. Note, also, that in many cases the organisation uses advertisements for job vacancies as general public relations exercises too. It represents another opportunity for that company to inform readers of its existence, what it is and does. If a logo appears in the advertisements, the kind of logo used can also be an indication of how the organisation sees itself.

The company may state that it is expanding, or may give that impression by advertising for a number of positions, perhaps in the same advertisement. This may give some notion of the possible promotion prospects too. Alternatively, the company may be contracting. Look carefully at anything in the advertisement which could indicate this and notice if any reasons for leaving are given for the last incumbent of the job.

If there is no company description, or if a box number is used instead of the name, you will need to ask yourself why that organisation is reluctant to publicise itself. Are they ashamed of who they are? Do they not want other employees to know that they are seeking more staff? Or that they are relocating? Or the rates of pay that they are offering in this instance?

14

The lack of company description on its own is not enough to make a reader suspicious – it may be omitted deliberately if the organisation is huge, well-known and any potential applicants should know of them and their business already.

On company philosophy, look for equal opportunity statements, etc. These vary enormously and you must consider how important these things are for you. The company may also use a sentence or phrase to sum up its place in the market, as in the Super Computer Systems example where the phrase 'technology at its best' was used. All these points help to indicate the type of organisation, structure and culture and how prestigious, bureaucratic, etc. the company is.

The name of the person you should reply to can also give you clues. Sounds unlikely? Look at the way the name is quoted – does the advertiser ask you to respond to David Coster? Or Mr. D. Coster? Or D. Coster, Personnel Manager? In other words, look at how formal the system seems, as this will tell you more about the organisational culture. In large organisations, recruitment and selection may be undertaken by a personnel department. Such advertisements may ask you to reply to the Recruitment Officer. In these cases, the selection processes are probably very well defined. If no name is given, this may be sloppiness on the part of the advertiser.

Media used

The position and medium used for the advertisement has not been considered so far. The size and place can give you further information. Even just thinking in terms of cost is useful – if the national newspapers are used, this is vastly more expensive than local advertising. It also gives an idea of whether the company is looking for a local applicant or is aiming to attract a nationwide response. Trade journals can also indicate the latter.

The amount that the organisation is willing to spend is worth knowing. Costs at recruitment agencies are often around 17–20% of the salary offered. The company then has many additional costs, such as temporary cover for the leaver, induction training for the new employee, etc. as well as obvious costs of advertising, interviewing, screening applicants with aptitude tests, etc.

Agency advertisements

The company has chosen to have the initial screening done by an outside agency. In this case, your aim must be to convince the agency that they should put you forward to the company. Sometimes, the agency carries out initial interviews and only submits the shortlist to their client. You may want to consider making your application a little more general if the agency handles many jobs in the industry in which you are seeking employment. In some cases you may think it more important to establish a rapport with the agency personnel rather than concentrating solely on the particular vacancy advertised.

Think about the reasons why any organisation uses agencies. Do they want specialists for whom that agency is known? Do they not have much expertise in that area themselves? This can be true when companies are seeking personnel at the top of a department, where there is nobody above with the kind of knowledge needed to recruit specialists. Companies who are trying to find staff from saturated labour markets may also choose this route as it saves them time and effort in screening a very large number of applicants.

Good advertisements are not just the right size (and in the right media on the right day), but are the right shape too. They have been professionally designed to attract the reader to the text, showing careful planning and thought. However, not all organisations either want or can afford this approach. Look for simple indicators too – is the advertisement boxed? Lineage advertisements in local papers may tell you that the company is small and unsophisticated in terms of recruitment. Look at how accurately the job is described – beware of those sounding too good to be true, few jobs live up to this.

Is this job special or are they covering up the boring parts? Try to find out what the drawbacks are. It will help you to decide whether to apply for the post and how to ask informed questions at an interview.

A few examples

FILM COMPANY REQUIRES SECRETARY

Excellent shorthand and typing skills are essential.
Must be able to work on own initiative.
Lots of common sense needed, with a sense of humour and low boredom threshold. The right person is more important than experience in the film industry.
Right salary for the right person.

Contact Jeremy on 01-111 1111.

(No agencies please)

This advertisement in a local paper gives a lot of information. Potential applicants need to look for 'estate agent'-type jargon.

The advertisement states that skills must be good (though without specifying the number of words per minute) and the second sentence implies that there will be low levels of supervision. Advertisements such as this often say that a sense of humour is required – assume that you'd need it! 'Low boredom threshold' is the real key. The typing and shorthand must be good, a sense of humour is required, with common sense and low boredom threshold – this all adds up to an organisation using the 'film industry' slogan to interest applicants in a boring, repetitive job. The glamorous image may hide the fact that the typist is needed to type lists of videos all day! With flexibility on salary and conditions though, a good typist may be able to make something of this position.

ENGINEERING STOREKEEPERS

A more exacting challenge . . .

When you're responsible for storing large numbers of parts for many different light engineering projects, ensuring a speedy and efficient supply becomes essential. If you have the confidence and ability to handle this, we'd like to hear from you.

The posts are based at our main Bracknell warehouses and will entail some shift working. Ideally, you should hold a full driving licence with HGV1 and fork-lift experience too.

In return, you'll enjoy a basic salary of £173.71 pw, plus £13,02 pw, in guaranteed bonus. The full range of benefits also includes contributory pension scheme and sports and social club.

If you're interested and would like to know more, please contact: Industrial Recruitment, C.M. Engineering, Staines Road, Bracknell, Berks. SL4 4TT, or telephone Bracknell (0344) 6666, quoting ref: LP216.

This advertisements speaks volumes! 'A more exacting challenge' means hard work, but the benefits are clearly set out. It is unlikely that these would be varied, as they obviously fit into the structure of a large company. Note that you are asked to quote a reference number – the industrial recruitment department may have many vacancies that they are attempting to fill.

You are told what the job requires in terms of driving licence, etc. but numeracy and literacy would also be required in good storekeepers, so that they can keep track of the many parts held, order more when running short and fill in the requisite forms.

The company name makes no statements about the organisation and the fact that the name is quoted in full and applicants are asked to respond to Miss Hetherington-Smith shows a formal approach. However, the company may change a little with the impact of new technology. The advertisement indicates that the advertiser is seeking a young person who can train in the wages office, and who will not command a large salary initially. It is unusual for a firm to quote conditions in such a formal way but then to say that salary is negotiable. It may not be – or there may be a system where salary rates are not published or made known to other employees.

The advertisement shows that a knowledge of both manual and computerised systems would be desirable, as well as specific details of PAYE and SSP. As the tasks involve payroll for manual staff, this indicates that the paint firm may have two payment systems, one for the semi-skilled craftsmen and another for the white collar workers.

Checklist

This section gives a checklist of factors to look at in the advertisement:

- *Where is the advertisement?*
- *Has it been placed by an agency?*
- *What does the company say about itself?*
- *What is the company's main product or service?*
- *What size is the company?*
- *How is the copy written (formally or informally)?*
- *Where is the job?*
- *How is the post described?*
- *What is the job title?*
- *Is the post for part of a team, or does the individual work mainly alone?*
- *What experience/qualifications are required?*
- *Will training be given?*
- *Does the advertisement ask for any personal qualities?*
- *Is salary stated?*
- *Are other benefits itemised?*
- *Are there any promotion prospects?*
- *How should you apply and to whom?*
- *Do you think that the advertisement oversells the job?*

3. Finding out more about the job and the company

The last chapter will have shown you how to begin to analyse an advertisement. You now have an idea of the organisational culture and a broad outline of what the company is looking for.

You must look at specific requirements of the job in more detail now, to find out what the employer is asking for and expecting.

About the job

This, of course is the most important aspect. When you have spent time studying the advertisement, you must look at the description of the job and the requirements to see whether you wish to apply.

Unless you have plenty of time, or are not in a hurry to change employment or are applying just to gain experience in applications and interviews, do not apply for positions that you know you will not be offered. Despite the abundance of time for those not in employment, a mounting pile of rejection letters is very damaging to morale and confidence.

Look at the way in which the job is described. If you have done similar work before, this should give you a good impression of the job content. If not, you will have to look more closely at the advertisement and talk to anyone you know who is already in that kind of employment. You may, for instance, be attempting to gain promotion. Find out how your own company assesses potential, if possible, and ask other people you know. This will help you to shape your application to the requirements and to show that you have the potential to succeed. It will also mean that the selection procedures do not come as a surprise and that you can be well prepared for each stage, thereby able to impress the prospective employer.

Look at *exactly* what the job asks for. If an advertisement cites five basic requirements and you have more than these, it will be worth applying (assuming that you want the job). If you have three out of the five, for instance, then you must assess the importance of the attributes you do and do not have. There may be some criteria which are mandatory and will not be waived, whilst others are desirable rather than necessary. You must also ask yourself whether it is likely that many candidates will have all the requirements. Look at the hidden requirements of the job and use your common sense! If an advertisement asks for Spanish 'O' level and you do not have this, you may still consider that your application may not be wasted if you can speak relatively fluently in that language. In many cases, qualifications requested give an indication of the general level required, but the interviewer may be forced to depart from the standards set if no suitable applicants are found. Your fluency in Spanish may actually be considered better than the 'O' level of another candidate if that was taken a long time ago and is now very rusty.

Remember too that in advertisements, the employer very often asks for all the characteristics and qualifications they would expect to find in an ideal applicant. Similarly, they may ask for the experience found in the last jobholder. These may be over-optimistic or no longer necessary for successful performance in that job. You must convince the employer of this if you intend to apply in these circumstances.

Look back at the sample advertisements in the last chapter. The Super Computer Systems company was looking for varied experience in domestic computer systems. Individuals with other backgrounds were also invited to apply. This type of advertisement indicates that a flexible approach would be used and there is very little that is explicitly requested. The organisation does not ask for ten years' relevant experience, or three. It leaves the individual to assess whether he/she has the qualities, background and experience to compete at that salary level. The advertiser wants the applicants to show that they have an understanding of the work and the industry, which would be shown by their applications. Only those candidates who feel fully confident of this (or those who have no idea and can be eliminated quickly) would put themselves forward.

The other sample advertisements are far more specific in their requirements. The film company was looking for a confident secretary, able to work largely unsupervised, with good shorthand and typing skills. Although good skills are deemed to be essential, the number of words per minute were not specified. Potential applicants with fast speedwriting rather than shorthand may also be considered. (However, if a particular type of shorthand is specified, this often means that the employer wants this so that it can be read back by others in the office and speedwriting would not be a viable substitute.) It is fairly clear that the company will not be happy with an individual whose secretarial skills have become rusty or who would need to ask lots of questions and expect full training.

In the advertisement for storekeepers, individuals who can operate stock control systems are sought. They would need to work methodically and systematically (being good at figurework), be able to keep their stores tidily and efficiently and perhaps use a computerised stock control system. They may be required to transport goods or to arrange for transfer to relevant depots, etc. The company may be prepared to train individuals or may require a thorough knowledge of machine parts, for instance, which may be similar in appearance or packaging.

In the example of the wages clerk, Brighton Paints were seeking a trainee with some knowledge of SSP and PAYE systems. They wanted somebody who had the potential to learn the new computerised systems (perhaps having worked with one before) and able to expand the role with the changing technology.

UNIVERSITY'S DEPARTMENT OF COMPUTER SCIENCE

requires an

EXECUTIVE OFFICER

A vacancy exists for a person with an interest in both financial management and computing. Suitable applicants may have experience in either discipline although a lively interest in both areas is desirable.

Duties will include the management and development of the computer system used for accounting and for processing purchase orders. The successful candidate will also be expected to produce financial reports and to liaise with senior staff for the preparation of estimates and financial strategy plans.

Applicants should have qualifications and/or suitable experience in either computing or business studies areas but the ability to communicate at all levels is also important.

Salary scale £9,500 – £11,000 depending on age and experience.

Applications should give full details of previous experience, qualifications and age together with the names of two referees and should be sent to: Mr. T. Trent, Dept. of Computer Science, University of North Wales, Wrexham, Clwyd. CH33 2ZZ.

The requirements of this job are:

- *experience in financial management/computing*
- *an interest in related areas*
- *relevant qualifications and/or experience*
- *understanding of accounts computing systems for purchasing, stock control packages, etc.*
- *ability to prepare budgets, estimates, plans etc.*

These are obvious requirements, but there are also hidden requirements:

- *ability to advise other senior staff*
- *interpersonal skills: communication – ability to inspire and persuade at all levels*
- *good report writing style – ability to translate financial strategies into comprehensive, informative bulletins/ narratives, etc.*

The advertisement does not ask for supervisory skills, but the successful applicant will have to make a case showing an ability to communicate complicated ideas effectively. Qualifications in either financial management, business studies or computing could be useful. A business studies graduate who has studied financial management, accounts and computing as part of the degree course would be in a strong position here, as this kind of course usually covers communication skills to.

The department is fairly bureaucratic and salary is dependent on *age* and experience. It is likely that they are seeking a new graduate – age is seldom asked in advertisements where the applicants are expected to be much older. Note that the requirement is for qualifications *or* experience, but as part of a university the philosophy of the organisation would probably be towards the former. The department may realise too that the salary offered would be insufficient to attract applicants who had both.

QUALITY CONTROL ENGINEER

An opportunity exists with Halcyon Acoustics Ltd. an experienced engineer.

We are a successful company engaged in the design and production of quality goods associated with amplification systems and noise control in industry.

The person appointed will report to the Quality Control Manager and will work closely with the production and design engineers. Duties will include maintenance of the current systems and making recommendations for new ones.

Applicants should hold appropriate qualifications in mechanical engineering and be familiar with design and manufacturing standards. A background in production management would also be helpful.

The position provides job satisfaction and opportunities for career progression. Apply to John Saunders, Halcyon Acoustics Ltd., Salford Road, Manchester. M34 1PP.

Requirements in this case are:

- *qualification in mechanical engineering*
- *understanding of design and manufacturing standards*
- *maintenance of production machinery*
- *application of quality control methods*

Also required though, are:

- *knowledge of this industry (and quality control and production methods within it)*

- *knowledge of updated or alternative production systems (you must show that you know the market and the costs of other machinery in order to be able to recommend better systems)*
- *ability to work in a team (liaising with peers in other departments)*

The position indicates a relatively high level of supervision (the successful candidate would work as part of a team, reporting to the manager). Maintaining systems and being familiar with manufacturing standards demands a methodical approach with attention to detail. As this individual would also have to recommend new systems, he/she must be able to provide evidence for this and make a good case.

The need to make recommendations on equipment shows that the company is changing. Note that the advertisement does not mention salary or conditions. The last sentence suggests that the company feels that the job is good enough to attract applicants irrespective of this. They are not seeking applicants motivated by the rewards, but by a 'job well done'.

DO YOU REALLY WANT TO BE RICH?

Our top consultants averaged £2,000 per month in February. We now have vacancies for trainee Sales Executives around the London area. No experience is necessary as training will be given. Bright personality and clean driving licence essential.

If you have the determination to earn these rewards and are available immediately, ring Geoff on 01-191 0022.

This is typical of many sales advertisements. Requirements are:

- *ability to communicate (sales training given, but shy, retiring types are unlikely to succeed)*

- *clean driving licence – willingness to travel and possibly to use own vehicle*
- *persistence to sell*

The advertisement includes very few actual requirements but many things can be deduced from it. The company does not describe itself or its products. A potential to sell (anything) is important. If the company had only to display its market-leading brand this would be stated and it might not need to pay large commissions to sales staff. The inference is that the salesman/woman would work hard for the rewards (note 'determination to earn…'). You would need a 'bright personality' (to sell a boring product?) too.

The company will provide training and is looking for potential, so applicants will not have to persuade the recruiter that all their background is relevant. Qualifications are not mentioned as verbal tenacity would be more important!

Such organisations often have a high labour turnover, as few individuals can tolerate pressure selling for long. For that reason, the company offers financial incentives to keep staff. Note that the advertisement says that the *top* consultants earned those amounts. Presumably the trainees would not.

More questions than answers

In the example shown opposite, it is evident that the position requires:

- *good typing and possibly audio/speedwriting*
- *good communication skills – to meet the many professionals and run the office*
- *driving licence and own transport (which presumably must be reliable!)*
- *organisational skills – both to be a good administrator and to run the office*
- *presentable appearance – meeting many clients/ professionals etc.*

This advertisement, however, raises many questions. It does not say what kind of office the successful applicant would be running and gives the impression that if a 'flexible approach' and driving licence is required, he/she could be asked to do just about anything. Certainly slavish adherence to a job description would not be expected here. There is also no indication of what the company business is.

Utopia Consultants are probably hoping to use this advertisement to attract many people, both for this job (if they get a large enough response, somebody should have the right background) and also for other jobs.

About the organisation

Look in your local library or telephone the company to ask for a copy of the annual report together with a job description and any promotional literature that they may produce. If you telephone, you must be prepared to be interviewed then. Many companies will want to obtain further information about you. They may want to advise you not to apply, or to encourage you after a discussion on your current and past employment. Be particularly careful if the advertisement requests a good telephone manner or good persuasive ability. Do not ring when you are likely to be overheard, when you are nervous or in a hurry. You may have to sell yourself and should be prepared for this. Also, anything that you say to the secretary will probably be repeated to the interviewer.

If the organisation is a small one and publishes no annual report, there are other ways in which you can find out about them. Your local library may have details of the Companies Register so that you can find out more.

There are other contacts too. Local newspapers or small trade journals where the job was advertised may be a source of information. You may be able to find out how often they advertise and for what other sorts of jobs. The media are not supposed to give confidential information about the companies which advertise with them, and should not be pressed for this. However, they may be able to tell you a little more about the organisation and would probably encourage you to apply so that the response to that advertisement is increased!

The local Jobcentre and careers service may also be a fount of knowledge. They will have many contacts with local employers and may be able to advise. A professional body or trade association may also be able to provide further details.

If you apply for a job near you, go to the company premises to look at the building and the people. An ideal time to go is either in the morning when work is beginning or at the end of the day. The way in which people enter and leave the building may tell you a lot about the organisation and the morale of the employees. If you are able to enter the premises, notice boards give a good idea of the company. They may be concerned with company rules and information, be filled with cartoons, or a cross-section of those with notices from trade unions, staff associations, individuals seeking accommodation, other vacancies within the company and newspaper cuttings etc.

If the company literature is sent to you automatically, this will tell you that the organisation is thorough and prepared. Ensure that you read all this before drafting your application. The company will expect you to be aware of all the information with which you have been provided and perhaps more.

Summary

1. *Find out about the company from annual reports, careers services and Jobcentres, or the Companies Register.*
2. *Analyse the type of organisation.*
3. *Look at the specific requirements of the job in terms of qualifications and experience needed.*
4. *Make deductions from the specific requirements to see what the implied requirements are.*

It is then up to you to decide if this job interests you enough to apply and whether you can satisfy enough of the selection criteria.

4. Drawing up your CV – the basic steps

The first thing to be said about this is that the information you give must be true. You should not limit yourself to one curriculum vitae however. As more and more people have access to word processors, many of your competitors will be designing their CV's and applications specifically for the post in mind – don't be left behind. Even if you do not have access to a word processor, you should not limit yourself. Have two or three CV's to choose from. This does not mean that you can leave out important details or lie about your experience, but the emphasis can alter according to the different posts and the points to be highlighted in each application.

The general format of a curriculum vitae covers the following:

- *personal details*
- *education and qualifications*
- *experience and details of career history*
- *personal interests, hobbies and pastimes*
- *other details*

Each of these is described in more detail with sample CV's at the end of the section.

Remember that brevity is important. The person who is screening the applications will want to be able to find the details easily and in a form uncluttered by irrelevant detail. You may well be able to write several pages on your virtues in your first post, but a potential employer will be interested in an informed synopsis – you can elaborate on all these details at an interview.

Your CV should be prepared as a rough draft to begin with. It is imperative that you allow enough time to plan it carefully and to play around with the information so that it is presented in the best way possible. If you are in any doubt, ask a friend or colleague to check it for you. Choose someone whose honesty you trust! Your assistance should ideally come from an individual who does not know your work or background particularly well. This will enable him/her to ask the sort of questions that would be raised by an outsider who did not know your business. It is very easy to slip into jargon or to assume that another person will understand what is meant. An independent, unbiased opinion will help to eliminate this.

Once you are happy with the draft CV, have it typed (see also the section on presentation) and make a master copy of each version.

Personal details

You should begin your CV by having the name that you are generally known by at the top. Put in your forename rather than just initials. You may want to add male or female if this is not necessarily apparent from the name. Your home address and telephone number (if you can be contacted there) should be clear, along with your date of birth. Remember to add the STD code for your telephone number as it is very irritating to have to keep looking this up. Quote your date of birth in words. This is particularly important if the company you are applying to is not British. Many other countries see 1.2.55 as 2nd January 1955 rather than 1st February. Optional extras include age, marital status, daytime telephone number, nationality and number of dependent children.

Your name and address are particularly important so that a potential employer is able to contact you. The date of birth is important for contracts and your pension rights, etc. Avoid putting in your title (Mr, Mrs, Miss, Ms, Dr, etc) as this can appear in your covering letter.

Put in your age with the date of birth if you think this would be helpful, but remember to alter it at each birthday!

If an advertisement asks for a young person, you may wish to put your age in (provided that you think you are!) or if age limits are quoted, if can be useful to save the reader from spending time calculating it. Individuals who are not so young may wish to avoid quoting their age if they feel that this would act as a bar. In these cases it may also be prudent to leave the date of birth off the CV – if an employer is serious this can be checked at an interview. However, candidates who do this may run the risk of being eliminated at an early stage because the recruiter cannot find the details easily and has many applications to scrutinise. On balance, it is best to leave it in unless you have had major problems related to this in the past.

Marital status and details of dependent children, sick fathers, etc. appear regularly in CV's but are rarely necessary. It is unlawful for an employer to discriminate on grounds of marital status and the employer is generally far more interested in what you can do for the company than the number, ages, sexes, etc. of your children. You may wish to bring the subject into conversation at an interview, but in most cases, this kind of detail absorbs valuable space on what should be a brief CV. Unless you intend to apply for a post where family stability is an important factor (in politics, or the forces for example, but who can guarantee that anyway?) it is usually wiser to omit this information.

Your nationality may be an important factor if you are applying for a post which is mainly based overseas or where you would be working under a work permit. If the latter is true, or you have been naturalised for only a short time, you may also want to include details of how long you have been resident in the country. Again, discretion is needed. This sort of information can emerge at an interview and takes up valuable space.

If you decide to include your business telephone number, also put in the extension if there is one. Only put these things in if you are prepared to be telephoned at work and will be in a position to talk freely.

Education and qualifications

The emphasis that you put on this section must reflect the degree of importance that it will have in helping you to get the job. In a sales environment, qualifications may be unimportant. For some companies and for the academic world in general, they can be critical. Similarly, the schools you have attended may be immaterial for a technical position in a provincial company, whilst those seeking employment in London's Stock Exchange may find that quoting the 'right' school makes all the difference. It is worth noting here that as an applicant, you must present yourself in as favourable light as possible despite what you may think of criteria such as these.

The section on education and qualifications may appear before that on career history or after it. If you have little employment experience but good qualifications, put the latter first. If you have been working for many years and your educational history is largely irrelevant, insert this after the section on background and experience. You must use all the information in a way which is most positive and relevant.

If you have attended a number of schools, either quote the one that you spent most time at, or say 'various schools'. Remember to put in the years in which you attended too (see examples). Do not put in the addresses of the schools, particularly if they are well-known. This uses up valuable space. If the potential employer wishes to take up educational references, addresses can be given at that time.

In some cases, education and qualifications can be condensed into the same section but this must not be at the expense of clarity. The reader must be able to see these details easily; they should not be mixed in together as in the example on the following page:

```
1968 - 74   Highlands School, St Helier, Jersey.
            'O' Levels in: Mathematics (grade B),
            English Literature (grade B), English
            Language (grade B), Geography (grade A),
            History (grade C), Commerce (grade A),
            French (grade C), Spanish (grade B),
            Economics (grade A)

1974 - 76   Devon Sixth Form College, Exeter, Devon.
            'A' Levels in: Geography (grade B),
            English (grade C), Economics (grade B),
            General Studies (grade C)

1976 - 80   University of Wales, Cardiff.
            2(ii) in Economics with special project
            in the history of economic thought.
            Also studied labour markets extensively.

1983 - 86   Kingston Polytechnic, Kingston, Surrey.
            Post-graduate Diploma in Management
            Studies with distinction
```

This fictitious candidate has good qualifications but has presented them badly. The highest qualifications should appear first, this is the one that an employer will be most interested in. The 'O' levels and their grades lose importance with higher qualifications gained and the distance of time.

This individual would be better advised listing educational establishments separately after the qualifications. The new format should look like this:

Qualifications

```
1986        Post-graduate Diploma in Management
            Studies, with distinction

1980        BA Economics (2ii)

1976        4 'A' levels in:  Economics, Geography,
            English and General Studies

1974        9 'O' levels in: Mathematics, English
            Literature, English Language, Geography,
            History, Commerce, Economics, French,
            Spanish
```

1983 - 86	Kingston Polytechnic, Kingston, Surrey (part-time)
1976 - 80	University of Wales, Cardiff, South Wales
1974 - 76	Devon Sixth Form College, Exeter, Devon
1968 - 74	Highlands School, St Helier, Jersey

This lists the qualifications in order of importance and avoids unnecessary details of specialist areas within the degree course (of course, if these are relevant to that application, they can be added or alluded to in a covering letter). The grades for the 'O' and 'A' levels have also been omitted as they are no longer crucial. Where grades are needed, the employer will ask.

The qualifications must be clear. If it is likely that the employer will not know what they are (this is particularly true of those gained overseas) or if the level will not be obvious, you should put in some explanation. It may be useful to note the equivalent, saying that a particular qualification is degree equivalent or whatever.

If you have taken an Open University degree or diploma, do not list all the subjects in which you obtained credits, but only the major stream.

It is important to specify when qualifications were taken – employers will want to know whether you were capable of sitting them all together (in 'O' and 'A' levels) and how long ago you studied. The gap between the DMS and first degree has been explained in this instance by the addition of the words 'part time' after Kingston Polytechnic.

If you have taken 'O' and/or 'A' levels a long time ago, the grading system may have changed. In some grading structures, for instance, 'O' level passes were quoted in figures 1 – 6, in some the grades were alphabetical and in some these were more arbitrary, eg. A, C and E were all passes, with F and H as fails. In the current system, A – C are passes, so that if you quoted an 'O' level grade E some time ago, it now looks like a fail. Make sure that any anomalies of this nature are explained adequately and if necessary offer to provide copies of your pass certificates.

Never quote primary or infant schools; these have no relevance to the employer. The grammar/secondary/ comprehensive or middle schools may also be left out if these add nothing to the application or were a very long time ago.

If you have studied for qualifications (once) but did not gain them, note this or there will appear to be a gap in the time between finishing education and your first employment, or whatever. This is particularly true for younger applicants where there were good mitigating circumstances surrounding the failures. This can be inserted in a positive manner by writing:

'studied for, but did not gain 'A' levels in …'

Employers may value the fact that your tutors thought you capable of studying at this level despite the results. Never lie about your qualifications as many employers will check or ask you for copies of the certificates.

Employment history

As with information on education and qualifications, begin with the most recent. Potential employers can become very irritated if they are forced to look through several pages and 20+ years of background before getting to the important part, ie. what you are doing now or have done most recently. Ex-service personnel are particularly prone to this.

You should give the most space to the job you have done most recently. Do not describe your first job in great depth if it was ten years ago. There must also be some balance in the length of the narrative for each job. Your last employment must contain the most information if this is the most senior.

The standard procedure is to catalogue your jobs in reverse chronological order, showing the name and business (where this is not obvious or well-known) of the employer, the dates of employment in months and years and the job title with a *brief* description of the salient duties and responsibilities. Do not use the tactic of listing the date, job titles and companies in one section followed by a longer piece of prose explaining what you did but running the duties in each position together. The material must be well organised so that it is easy to follow. You can show *(briefly)* the achievements and strengths in each position with a note of your contributions to the profit if this is applicable.

The exact address of the organisation is not needed although it is helpful to give the area. As with other details, the recruiter will ask if necessary or you may wish to include this as a reference (precise details can then be given, but at a later date). Addresses, in this context, also waste space which could be more profitably used to convince the reader that you merit an interview.

Some people do not name their company – this is not recommended. It conveys the impression that they are ashamed of it and makes it harder for the person assessing the application to obtain a 'feel' for what the individual was doing. Many things are deduced by the reader, taking into account the job title, the company business and size and the list of your duties. These things all contribute to helping to build up a picture of the sort of work undertaken and leaving out the company name denies the reader some of that information.

You will not need to give details of the grades of your previous positions. This would be irrelevant to a new employer and in any case the recruiter is unlikely to know the details of the grading structure of your past employers. Although you may have been in a high grade, omit details of this. Ensure instead that you put in information on any promotions that you gained. You may also want to mention merit increases gained, although this may be done through the covering letter rather than the curriculum vitae.

In cases where you have undertaken a number of similar jobs, amalgamate these into one section if this is feasible.

Give a brief outline of the duties with the caveat that you had similar employment in those companies and give inclusive dates. Thus, a section of the CV would appear in the following format:

```
May - Oct 1979   Jeffrey Smith and Sons, Catering
                 Assistant
                 Whilst in this post, I obtained my
                 diploma in catering and undertook
                 duties such as menu planning for
                 the staff canteen (1000+ diners
                 daily), preparation of some dishes,
                 ensuring cleanliness of the canteen
                 area and dining rooms etc. etc...

Oct '79 - Jan '80   Frederick Lion Catering Co Ltd
                    Duties mainly as above, with
                    occasional preparation of buffets
                    for conferences

Jan '80 - Aug '80   JFC Hotels Ltd
Aug '80 - Sept '82  Industrial Foods Ltd
Sept '82 - Sept '83  Worley Hospital (NHS)
                    In each of these positions, I was
                    engaged on a temporary basis as a
                    Canteen Assistant.  Duties were
                    similar to those outlined for
                    Jeffrey Smith & Sons.  In addition
                    I undertook ordering of non-
                    perishable goods for the kitchens
                    at Frederick Lion.
```

Similarly, if you have had a period of time which does not advance your career and in which you did a number of different things, this can be described as follows:

```
April '84 - Aug '87   During this time I undertook
                      various temporary assignments
                      in addition to travelling
                      around South East Asia and
                      nursing a terminally ill
                      relative.  One temporary
                      assignment during this period
                      was for 10 months at ....
```

The object of condensing these types of activity is to avoid giving the impression that you are unstable whilst giving legitimate reasons for the activity.

Exactly how to describe the duties you have undertaken is explained in the later chapter on beating the opposition.

Other information

It is usual to put in a section on hobbies, pastimes and personal interests. This section can be used for charity work or personal achievements too (preferably relevant). One word to cover each of these is sufficient, eg. 'ballroom dancing' is enough – do not be tempted to inform the reader that in 1986 you obtained the gold medal in ballroom dancing and bronze in tap dancing, etc. If this information is relevant you will have included it in the sections on duties and responsibilities. Details of your hobbies should not swamp the CV so that it looks as if you have no time left for work.

You may also wish to use this miscellaneous section to insert details such as:

- *full clean driving licence*
- *languages*

Notice the distinction between skills (things you can *do*) and interests (things that you are enthusiastic about and enjoy). 'Football' on its own conveys nothing – you should tell the reader whether you play well (you may be a member of a local football team for instance) or whether you confine your interest to spectating, or whether you do both. See the later notes on this and remember the golden rule 'only put it in if it is relevant'.

You must be able to talk about anything you include in this section just as well as you can about your work. The interviewer will also note the type of activities you include to give an idea of your personality. If you have a balance of sporting, passive and social interests, aim to show this. You may be asked to justify these. Knitting may be a laudable and interesting pastime but may seem incongruous for a job that requires a dynamic individual. If you *are* dynamic, but have that kind of interest, emphasize that this is how you 'unwind' and relieve the stresses of the day. Similarly, if you have a very sedentary job, the sporting interests may indicate that the personality balance is maintained.

Avoid references to your religion or politics unless you *know* that this will help your application, eg. saying that you have been treasurer for your local political group when applying for employment at the party headquarters, or stating religious denomination where the charity you are applying to is known to favour that, etc.

The last section of your CV can also include a note regarding references being available on request, medical details, short courses undertaken, publications produced etc. Put these in only where relevant, and see the later section on these.

Lastly, you may wish to mark your CV 'Confidential'. In most organisations this should not be necessary as all recruiters should treat these with respect and discretion.

Checklist

Personal details
1. *Is your name clear?*
2. *Is the address clear? Have you remembered to include the postcode?*
3. *Is the STD code included in the telephone number?*
4. *Have you put in your correct date of birth? Is your age still correct?*
5. *Have you stated whether you are male or female, if this is not clear from your name?*

Education and qualifications
1. *Have you listed your qualifications clearly with the highest first?*
2. *Will the employer know what level your qualifications are?*

3. *Where grades are quoted, have you been consistent?*
4. *Is the section well spaced so that each qualification is easily seen?*

Employment history

1. *Have you listed your employment history in reverse chronological order?*
2. *Is the name of the employer and the nature of the business clear?*
3. *Are the dates given in months and years? Have you made sure that any gaps are adequately explained?*
4. *Have you put in more about your current post than the others?*
5. *Do the sections give a fair summary of your main duties and achievements?*
6. *Have you included relevant details of machines that you can operate?*

Other information

1. *Can you talk about the hobbies which you have quoted?*
2. *Have you given an idea of the level of your interest?*
3. *Is it clear whether these show skills or just enthusiasm?*
4. *Have you balanced the interests?*
5. *Have you ensured that the CV is not swamped by your hobbies?*
6. *Have you added extra information, such as driving licence, languages, computer literacy, etc?*

5. CV's – Presentation and common problems

In addition to designing several versions of your CV, it may be useful to do them in differing lengths. The basic rule, as always, is 'keep it brief', but many CV's bear a note to the effect that further details can be provided. If the prospective employer seems interested, you are then in a position to supply extra information. The supplementary CV may be longer than the basic but should not exceed four or five sides. The 'ordinary' CV will be between one and three sheets long, but adding extra information should not do more than double the length.

It is possible to make a CV interesting and informative despite the brevity – you must work at this, eliciting the help of friends and advisers if necessary. However, CV's written by specialist consultants have a recognisable format. If you take their advice, you should then write your own CV in your own style and wording.

Do several drafts of your CV before having it typed. Then check again to ensure that the spacing looks right and that everything can be seen easily and clearly.

Your CV must be sent out in pristine condition, folded as few times as possible. Black lines at the edge of the page from photocopying detract from the appearance of the CV, as do smudges. Remember that this is especially important if the positions you intend to apply for call for neatness and attention to detail.

Curriculum vitae should always be typed (professional typesetting tends to put employers off), should be well spaced out so that the information is clear and readable and should have nothing crossed out. Type on one side of the page only. If you need to change your CV, make sure that you do this properly. Last minute changes, crossings out and white-outs are not acceptable.

Keep your curriculum vitae flat. CV's must be sent uncrumpled, not straight from the filing cabinet and omitting the last job. An old CV *will not do*. You must take your potential employer as seriously as you expect them to take you. Covers and flashy folders to hold the CV's tend to irritate rather than impress potential employers. Well typed CV's are fine; they do not need to be expensively produced.

Spelling and grammar

These are perennial problems in CV's. Whether you are sure of your spelling or not, ask someone else to check as it is very easy to miss typographical errors. 'Liaise' is one word that is used frequently in CV's and is often misspelt. Also often misspelt are words like mathematics, programme, pursue, procedure and maintenance. Make sure that you have not fallen into these common traps. Choose your words carefully too, notice the difference between infer and imply, affect and effect, principles and principals, continually and continuously, etc. You must also ensure that you use the correct part of the verb for the person, not 'they was', for example.

Grammar is important too. Most business communications are written, so the employer will want to be sure that you can write grammatically. If you are not sure that your command of English is sufficient, ask others for help or use a good book. Your library should stock many books on the subject.

Sentences and style

Your sentences should not be too long. Brevity is the key word here too. Many people insert phrases in the text rather than sentences; this is not recommended, do not forget the verb. Often CV's appear to be written in note form too, again not advised. An example of this is:

Responsible for 3 staff. Had control of £x of capital expenditure.

A paragraph or two is all that is needed to describe each job on your CV. Note that the purpose of a new paragraph is to cause a break in the text when changing the subject, or introducing a new factor. Do not be tempted to start a new paragraph because the last seems too long. Precis it instead. Similarly do not include all the facts together in one paragraph if the job or subject clearly has two quite different aspects.

Avoid gimmicks in general. These may add to the novelty value of the application but rarely win respect. Gimmicks are usually a waste of your time, effort and money. Designing a jigsaw-like CV if you wish to work in a toy company may seem an original idea but is not guaranteed to impress the prospective employer if it is hard to read and harder still to put back together when dropped!

CV's have also been designed where the text is written in a spiral – original but irritating and time consuming to read.

This is my
curriculum vitae,
saying the most
wonderful things
about me and my
career to date.
But it is doubtful
whether anyone
will take the
time and trouble
to read it!
This is one case
where originality
does not
pay!

Layout

CV's come in all shapes and sizes, may be expensively produced on glossy paper or scruffily put together on one or two sheets of flimsy A4 paper, or found in illegible screed on quarto sized note paper.

It is very rarely worth including a photograph. This is an American habit which does not usually find favour in the United Kingdom. Photographs tend to turn the CV into an object of curiosity. They do not reproduce well and often mar a CV which would otherwise appear well-presented.

Ideally your CV should be produced on A4 paper as most companies deal mainly with this size. It is therefore less likely to get lost in other filing or to become damaged if the length overhangs all the other papers.

The curriculum vitae must be brief, informative and clear. In order to add clarity, ensure that sections on different topics do not run into each other. The reader will be looking for name, age, qualifications and experience at the first glance. This means that these parts of the CV must be easily located.

Divide the CV into the relevant compartments so that it is visually easy. Do not cram information into a small space in an effort to cut down the length of the CV – summarise the data instead. Put dates in the left hand margin (month and year only) and make sure that these are easy to follow. Use the tabulator on your typewriter or word processor for this.

The format of your CV should look something like this:

```
Personal details

   Name
   Address and telephone number
   Date of birth and age
   Marital status  )  optional
   Nationality     )

Education and Qualifications

Date           Qualifications  Educational
(month and     obtained        establishment
year)
```

You may wish to include professional qualifications in here as well as basic education.

Alternatively, divide this section into two – Education and Qualifications – as shown earlier. For senior managers and staff it may look more professional to put the career and employment history first as this is more relevant.

Employment History

```
Date    Company name    Job title and brief
        and business    description of role
```

Begin with the most recent position, which should have the longest description.

Interests and hobbies

Keep this part very brief, just the name of the pastime with no description. Do not include anything that you are not prepared to talk about at an interview and remember that the interviewer may not pick your favourite of the subjects on your list. If you like swimming, horse riding, reading novels and theatre going but decide to add voluntary work for good measure, be sure that the interviewer will choose that to ask you about!

In some cases, individuals head their CV's 'Curriculum Vitae'. This is a matter of preference and perceived organisational culture. The reader will know what the information comprises if it is properly laid out. However, in more bureaucratic organisations, this heading is sometimes preferred. Use your discretion – it will seldom make any difference to your application, but omitting it can save space.

The format of CV's varies enormously. That described above is only one way of compiling it. Layouts may change according to the length and type of information inserted. For example, the beginning of a CV can be set in different ways:

```
              CURRICULUM VITAE

           Mary Jane Bloggs
   21 The Fields, Campton Bleckett, Herts
              SG44 3UX

         C Bleckett 2178915

              -------
```

Or:

```
Name:   MARY JANE BLOGGS    Date of Birth: 31.08.42

Address: 21 The Fields      Age:  45
         Campton Beckett    Married with 3 children
         Herts SG44 3UX     Nationality: British

Tel:    0244-2178915
```

As you can see, data can be blocked or indented and centred. There are no set rules on this – you must see which looks better to you taking into account the material you will include. Stick to the same style throughout though, do not change format within the same CV. You may consider that putting in 'name:' and 'address:' etc is unnecessary as this is obvious. Use your discretion here, decide which looks best and makes the most effective use of the space.

You may wish to use coloured paper (not too bright). Many individuals in public relations use yellow paper as this has been found to be noticed most. Use discretion though, vivid colours, particularly under fluorescent lights, can be a strain on the eyes of the reader and make your CV hard to read. Think about the person receiving it. In a fast moving design company it may be imperative to find an eyecatching way of presenting and selling yourself.

Keep to the same typeface throughout the CV. If you are using a good typewriter or word processor, it may be possible to use bolder print for headings so that they stand out. Whatever script you use, ensure that the style and size will be easy to read.

Common problems

One of the commonest problems with curriculum vitae is inattention to small details. Do remember to put in your date of birth – and do not accidentally insert the year in which you are writing the CV! It is amazing how many applications are received from people who, according to their CV's, are not yet born or only months old.

Problems of spelling have been addressed previously. Checking this is imperative. Typographical errors also creep in easily. You should check the CV line by line and word by word as well as asking others to glance over it. Ensure that you use the correct words – one howler in a CV said that the applicant had not taken 'A' levels because there was no 'pacific' reason for it! The writer actually meant 'specific' of course, but as the word is often mispronounced, the error was compounded in writing.

Common problems also include those in length and style. These things *must* be geared to the sort of job and the organisation. For instance, it is no good telling a banking organisation in depth about your drama qualifications and acting ability if the employer is likely to want a calm individual to work methodically in an accounting function. Think of the image that you are portraying. It is a common problem to expand at length to the detriment of the space in which you could tell the employer about what you can offer in terms of the *work*. Fit the CV style to the job.

Gaps in career or employment history are also abundant in applications. *Do* explain gaps or the cynical reader may think that you were in prison! (See later notes on special cases if you were.) If you stopped work to study on a full time basis, make sure that the reader does not have to flick backwards and forwards through the details of the CV to deduce this. A note at the relevant chronological point saying that you had returned to full time study is all that is needed eg:

Sept '85 – June '86 Full time study – see section on education

You do not need to repeat the detail. If you were out of the country or had several temporary posts, condense thse periods together as mentioned in the section on employment history earlier.

Many people also forget to put in any detail of the companies that they have worked for. The entry in the CV may appear as six months spent with J.J. Smith and Sons Ltd. and three years with Hamish Octagons followed by five and a half years at Garfield, Nelson and Chambers. Although the recruiter may have an idea of the business (for instance, Garfield, Nelson and Chambers may sound like a firm of solicitors or estate agents), but it is useful if the employer actually *knows* what the nature of the business is. The description of the post will give some information and some can be guessed, but the last thing you want is for the reader of the CV to have to spend time guessing and getting irritated, so remember to put this in. One line or word may be all that is needed, eg J.J. Smith and Sons Ltd., local builders, and Hamish Octagons, construction agents, but this is sufficient to convey an idea of the nature and size of the business.

Checklist

1. *Is the curriculum vitae as brief as possible?*
2. *Is it on A white or pale paper?*
3. *It is clear and well spaced? Can all the information be found easily?*
4. *Are there any smudges or black lines on the copies? (If so, copy again, use 'white-out' for smudges or retype.)*
5. *Have you checked the CV for spelling, grammatical and typographical errors? Has this been double-checked by someone else?*
6. *Have you kept to the same style and typeface throughout?*

6. CV's – The extras

There may be other items that you feel are pertinent and wish to add to your CV. Some people add details of their career aims – this is useful if you are submitting an unsolicited CV. You may want to specify the areas and company locations in which you are prepared to work. This is better done in a covering letter though, rather than taking up space on the CV. You should avoid sections on personal characteristics – these will be seen at an interview and statements such as 'I get on well with people' and 'I'm a jolly person' just sound crass.

You should also consider adding data on any special skills that you have but which are not related to your job. An example of this would be aptitude and proven ability with computers, even though your job does not involve you in this.

The notes below give some guidance on possible additions.

Medical details

Unless you have had a serious illness which you feel that potential employers should be aware of, omit this. The recruiter will assume that you are in good health unless you state otherwise.

If you have a gap in your employment history due to time spent in hospital, or you were away from work due to a serious illness, etc. then it may be wise to explain separately that you are now in good health and have no recurring problems. In instances where there are still problems, you should specify the extent to which they do or do not affect your job. Be honest but positive – say what you are capable of and leave the negative side if possible. Do not lie about your medical history as your contract may be based on the details in your CV. The details can all be explained at an interview and you would have an opportunity to put your case fully then.

Employers with over 20 employees are required by law (1944 Disabled Persons (Employment) Act) to employ three per cent of disabled persons in the workforce. However, the act deals only with those who are registered disabled and is very difficult to enforce. If you are registered disabled, declare this and give some details of your disability. Again, you must remember to emphasize what you *can* do rather than the problems that you have encountered. If the company has over 250 employees it is required to issue a policy statement in its annual report which may prove helpful (see the section on finding out more about the company).

Salary details

This is another detail which can generally be omitted, particularly where your employment history spans a number of years. The payments you received a decade ago are rarely relevant to the potential employer. If you are earning a high salary and do not wish to waste your time if the employer will not pay more than this, put a note to that effect in the covering letter rather than inserting salary details in your CV. Giving details of the salary that you are seeking can limit your negotiating strength later on though.

If your present salary is very good, but you would still wish to be considered for the job if the salary was less, you should also leave out details of your current salary. If you put in any reference to your remuneration, the reader may decide in advance that you would not accept the job and reject you before you have a chance to decide for yourself.

If your current salary is poor in terms of the market rates, the reader may want to know why. Your organisation may pay badly (or you may have quoted only the basic rate which did not take into account bonus payments etc). The reader will very often not ask though, and reject you on the assumption that you are not worth more!

Languages

Quote languages that you can speak or write only if this seems pertinent to the employment you are seeking and only if you have a reasonable ability. Rusty school French will not impress anyone if it has no relevance to the position you are seeking or to the organisation. However, if say, you are fluent in German and the company has a large German subsidiary company, this may be useful.

Naturally, the above will not apply if you wish to be appointed as a translator and have already given full details of your ability and competence in your chosen language(s). Use your discretion.

Driving licence

As with the example above, include this only if it is relevant. For anyone whose job involves a company car, or travelling widely, it certainly will be. You should specify how long you have held a clean licence, when you started driving and state that you have had no accidents if this is the case.

Most sales representatives will want to include this as will those who can see that the next promotion would gain them a company car!

Short courses

If you have taken a number of these, they may merit a separate section of the CV. You should include only those useful for the job and which show your commitment to keeping updated in your field of work.

If you have taken very many short courses, you may wish to state that some of the courses you have been on include … Whilst you want to look enthusiastic, you do not want the prospective employer to think that you will be demanding to go on lots of courses as soon as you arrive, so too many may look threatening!

Be careful too, in including trade union sponsored courses – this makes many employers (except for the trade unions etc!) hesitant. Remember that this is a sensitive issue and you will have to exercise your judgement in deciding whether this would seem acceptable to the prospective employer. Your motives may be pure but they can be easily misunderstood.

Publications

Again, the key word is relevance. A list of items which you have had published may be useful if you are an academic, researcher or journalist, etc. You should aim to keep this selective though, including just a few of the articles or books or whatever. Give the title of the piece, the name of the magazine or journal that it appeared in where applicable and the date. State that you have listed only a representative sample of your works and stick to the more recent ones if possible.

References

Omit these unless you are specifically asked for them. If you feel uncomfortable without some reference to them, say that references can be provided.

Where you are asked to give references, use your most recent or current employer if possible and the one immediately prior to that. If this is impossible because the company is no longer in existence, or has been taken over etc, state this and give the last possible one. If your last company went out of business but you have a reference from them, attach this, but again *only when requested to do so*. If you are applying for your first job, be prepared to use a tutor at your school, college or university. Do not include character witnesses or personal referees unless asked. Many employers would be put off by receiving gushing letters extolling your virtues whilst telling them nothing of how you would perform in the job.

Whenever you do have to give the names and addresses of referees, make sure that you have asked the individuals first if they are willing to do this. Ask them what they are willing to say about you before you quote them as referees.

References are usually only taken up after an interview. If one of your references is liable to be less than enthusiastic about you, say so at the interview and explain why. Try to minimise the problem, indicating perhaps that whilst you generally got on well with your boss and colleagues, there was one specific incident that marred your time there, or whatever. If you think that your boss will give a bad reference to prevent you from leaving, say so but handle this carefully and be prepared to back up this with evidence of your own good work; perhaps you have been told by others that your work is good or gained a special merit payment etc. These things can be used to back up your case but should not be overplayed.

Reasons for leaving

Again, omit this unless it is a burning issue or there is a gap in time since your last employment. It is sad but true that it is easier to find a job from a job than from unemployment.

At all costs, avoid reasons for leaving such as 'personality clash' which instills the fear that you are impossible to work with. This is especially true where a position calls for good communication skills and liaison with others. A potential employer seldom really believes that everybody else hated you, your last boss too, even though it was bad enough to make you leave.

You will find more details on this topic in the section on application forms as they frequently ask for this information.

Hobbies and pastimes

Think about what you intend to include here and the sort of thing that will be seen as acceptable. Watching television may be your favourite pastime, but this rarely impresses recruiters. Remember to quote only those things that you can talk about at an interview. If you mention an overriding interest in waterskiing no interviewer will be impressed to hear that you have actually only done this once, on holiday in Spain five years ago. Include things that you have done recently and be careful – you may find that the interviewer is knowledgeable about your chosen hobby, so do not bluff.

Try to list just a few interests which show a balance. An individual who appears from the curriculum vitae to do bookkeeping all day and stamp collecting all evening will not look very sociable on paper! Similarly, if you have a pressurised post or one in which you have to be very outgoing, find a way of showing that you do take part in relaxing activities too. Do not give the impression that you cannot 'turn off' or 'wind down' after work and that you are heading for a breakdown!

Don't fall into the trap of saying that you like meeting people without putting it into context. Show what kind of activities you take part in for this, eg. 'I find meeting people very rewarding and do so twice a week when I visit the local old people's home'. This example is rather long though and if you can put in single words to cover your interests, do so.

Try to balance your interests without distorting the truth, so that you have one or two sports, one or two quieter or more passive interests and something to show your interest in other people, eg voluntary or community work where this is applicable. If one of these areas does not interest you at all, or you *hate* sport, for instance, do not put in something just to add the balance. There may be sufficient in the things that you have already put into the CV.

In general, keep the section on hobbies and pastimes short, do not use this as padding. Indicate also what level of interest you have, whether this is something that you do very well in a competitive sense or whether it is something that you just enjoy at a sociable level and like doing.

Career summaries

If you have done several different jobs but wish to show a link between them and a natural progression (the aim of a good CV), you can include a career summary. This is often included for more senior positions where the recruiter wants to find an instant overview before looking at the detail of the individual's posts.

The career summary is literally just that. It should precis the skills that you have acquired and give just an *outline* of your capabilities. It is usually put into the CV just after the personal details and before the core of the CV.

Career summaries are explored in more detail in the section on angling your experience to fit the vacancy.

Service experience

If you have had a long and distinguished service career, you may want to add a section on this. Keep it brief unless you know that the company you are applying to is particularly interested in this. This kind of section may be of more use if the service experience was a long time ago, otherwise it can be included in the general employment history section.

Professional qualifications

If you have taken any professional qualifications, you may wish to put in a separate section to cover these. You should only do this if there are several to quote and/or these cover different fields of work. You must also ensure that the levels of these are clear so that any reader understands where these fit into academic levels.

7. CV's – Special points

This chapter deals with special points for specific types of applicant. This can be used in conjunction with the chapter on angling your experience to fit the vacancy and it aims to add some useful points in specific cases.

Advice from specialist consultants is always helpful but you should aim to design your own CV as those from consultants often fit a standard recognisable pattern. This on its own would not necessarily count against you, but it is obviously better to give the impression that your application is your own unaided work and is a planned but still spontaneous reaction to the advertisement.

Remember to utilise the points already made but take into account your own particular circumstances. The sections below give some guidance on things to remember but are not exhaustive. Conversely, do not feel that you need to include references to everything mentioned in the special sections which apply to you – use your discretion and be selective in the points that you include. Brevity is still important, particularly for those with no previous work experience.

Advice to school leavers

This section will encompass not only school and college leavers, but all those with no previous paid full-time work experience. The absence of the part of the curriculum vitae which deals with employment history should enable you to keep the document even more brief than is otherwise the case. One side of A4 paper should be sufficient.

Make sure that if you include grades of your qualifications, you include all of them. Employers will spot the applicants who list only the good grades and omit to mention others. If your grades are not very good overall, omit them – the employer will ask for details if these are needed. See the notes in the section on qualifications in the chapter on basic steps, and note that any grade changes may have to be explained if the grading structure has altered, eg if you had an 'E' grade which was a pass on the old system, you will have to say so as at the time of writing most 'O' level boards only gave A, B or C grades for passes. Also, if you have obtained several qualifications in the same subject, you may not need to indicate this. In many cases, secretarial colleges enter their students for RSA examinations in shorthand and typing at several different speeds on the same day. If this was the case for you and you obtained speeds of 70, 80 and 90 words per minute together, omit references to the first two.

If you do have any kind of work experience, you may feel inclined to list everything. The advantage of this is that the employer can see that you have some knowledge and understanding of what the world or work is about. However, many people in this position fall into the trap of putting in irrelevancies too – the two week job as a temporary secretary or three weeks spent bricklaying. If you have nothing else, put these in but try to keep to relevant experience if possible. If you are applying for a job as a clinical chemist, the three weeks spent on a building site is highly irrelevant. However, if you are applying with the intention of becoming a trainee surveyor or even an architect, it can be seen as valuable.

If you have taken part in work experience programmes organised by your school or a Youth Training Scheme, give details of the relevant parts and try to show what you gained from the experience. If you can show that you progressed in this situation and that specific work was channelled to you, do so. The YTS programmes should help you to isolate your transferable skills; that is, what you have done that would be of value to an employer. If you have a good grasp of figures and can understand stock control systems, or you know the basics of computer programming, indicate this too.

Similarly, make the link between your hobbies and personal qualities which show your skills and aptitudes. If you are secretary to a local youth group or can show organisational skills of this nature, it can be very helpful. You may have been treasurer for a local charity, showing that you are competent in handling money. This type of activity also reinforces your image as an honest person who can be trusted.

Try to avoid quoting too many interests or giving the impression that you flit from one pastime to another. You have had no work experience so the employer is likely to be more than usually concerned that you will settle into the working environment without giving up. Employers will be impressed by a keen attitude, a willingness to work hard and progress within the company and an attitude which shows 'staying power'. That means you will not be consistently unpunctual, take days off or just get fed up and leave. As mentioned earlier, recruitment is expensive and employers take proportionately more of a risk with individuals who have never worked than with those who have some (even if limited) proven ability.

If you have been involved in student politics, be careful how you mention this. Positions which show status, such as President of your branch of the National Union of Students (NUS), are just about permissible, but avoid mentioning political parties. You *must* avoid sounding too political or a 'do gooder'. Note, too that some employers still see universities as 'hotbeds of communism'. If your involvement is limited to a junior role within the NUS, emphasise this and state that this was during your first year or whatever. Minimise third and fourth year activities of this sort as employers tend to think that you should have been studying during your final year!

Involvement with the entertainments committee shows sociability and organisational skills. Similarly, involvement with student newspapers shows communication skills and should be included.

After unemployment or redundancy

If you have never been employed, see the section above. The main problem you will encounter is explaining the gap in your employment and showing that you are still employable. At all costs you must avoid giving the prospective employer the impression that you feel hard done by or have a chip on your shoulder. Employers want to take on cheerful employees, not those still disgruntled and harbouring past resentments. Find a way of releasing your feelings of anger, rejection and depression elsewhere. It may be more difficult for you to give the impression that you are specifically interested in *this* job with *this* company when you know that you are desperate for work and will take any job offered.

If you have been made redundant, try to show that you understand the company's rationale behind the reorganisation or whatever. This creates a feeling that you are loyal to the companies that you work for. If the organisation went out of business, show that your attitude to this was responsible and do not let the reader of your curriculum vitae think that this was in any way due to you. This can be more difficult than it sounds if you were involved in the financial side of the company or in business planning, but it is important, so work at it!

Show that you have utilised the unsavoury experience by doing something positive which will help you in your future career. Some people learn languages etc., but this is often not directly relevant. You must give the impression that the time has been planned carefully. Be specific too (though again, without sounding desperate for the job) – show that the activities you have been pursuing were geared towards just the sort of employment that you are now applying for, in their sort of company. If you have undertaken formal training to prepare for a career change or advancement, be specific in how that training fitted the job applied for. (It is worth noting that research shows it is far more difficult to change career in a move from one organisation to another than to be transferred within a company. Also, progression up the career ladder is more difficult directly after redundancy or unemployment.)

If you are circulating many unsolicited applications, you must still tailor these to the organisations and the kinds of job that you are interested in there. Your application is wasted without this. In unsolicited applications ask if they have any current vacancies for the sort of post you are seeking, or whether their future planning indicates that any may be available in the near future. This tactic is allied to the classic 'alternative close' in selling, giving the reader a choice of whether to consider you now or consider you later, rather than not at all.

Remember, too, your most positive points, including the ability to begin work immediately. This can be a very valuable plus-point in your application.

After career breaks

If you have had a career break to raise a family or are changing career direction, it can be very difficult to convince a prospective employer that you are serious about the post and are committed to it.

Your career change may be due to circumstances beyond your control, if you were a dancer but injury prevents you from continuing with this for instance. You must work hard to find transferable skills. In the example above, the individual may be able to utilise a knowledge of physiology and anatomy, or may go into a related field such as theatre administration. This would obviously be an easier and more logical change than into a general office job. In this sort of position, you must highlight the strands of your career that always showed competence in that field and weave these in with your future aims. Find evidence of continuity. If you have undertaken retraining, sound positive about this, indicate that it was thorough and that you took it seriously.

If you are returning to work after a career break to raise a family, you must convince the employer that you are now firmly committed to working and that you have a real interest in their field of work. Cite any refresher courses that you may have taken and emphasize, without labouring the point, that your child care arrangements are adequate and that you will not be pining for your children when at work. This may sound patronising and unnecessary, but is aimed at helping you to convince the recruiter that you are a sound investment as an employee. If you are returning to work after looking after dependent relatives, the same applies.

If you are returning to work after a spell in prison, note the Rehabilitation of Offenders Act, 1974. This covers people with certain past convictions but who have not been convicted again for specified lengths of time. After these trouble-free periods, the individuals are deemed to have 'spent' their convictions and do not have to declare them. Your library will have full details of this and many advice centres can give further information to clarify this. It is illegal for an employer to discriminate on the grounds of the conviction if this should be 'spent'. However, this is very difficult to prove.

If the conviction has no bearing on your prospective employment and you can avoid mentioning it, do so. You must not lie about it though and may have to declare it if asked. It is relatively easy to leave this off CV's, but some application forms require details of convictions. If you put down this period as unemployment on your CV, remember that an interviewer may ask about your attempts to obtain work during that period.

Employers may well respect your honesty if you declare this time, but you must weigh this up against possible suspicion that could be felt. Advice from the Manpower Services Commission's rehabilitation and resettlement section could also be helpful.

If you are returning to employment in the United Kingdom after working abroad, you must show how the position you held abroad was similar to the kind of job done here. The recruiter must be persuaded that the change in culture would not mean that your training and abilities have a completely different slant. You may be able to stress the positive side of this too, emphasising your increased awareness of international business or whatever.

If you have worked overseas, references may be difficult for the employer to follow up. Testimonials can be helpful here, provided they are translated into English if necessary and say sufficiently good things about you. Like open references, the very fact that they are open means that they must be very good to be of any value. If they are translated, make sure that the translation is authenticated by a reputable source.

Women

You may think it unnecessary to have a special section devoted to women as they make up half the working population, but there are special points to be considered.

Despite the sex discrimination legislation, women still have a hard job sometimes in convincing employers of their loyalty. Many recruiters see women as carers; if you have children, find a way of emphasising (again, without labouring the point) that your child care is adequate, that you do not end up taking days off from work, that you can be mobile if the post demands this and are able to work late to finish important tasks when the demand arises. It may seem grossly unfair that women are forced to explain and defend constantly, but it may help to get them to the interview stage, where they are more able to persuade the employer.

If you are in an age group where the employer thinks that you will leave to have a family, scotch this point before it arises. Indicate that this is not appropriate at the moment, perhaps by saying that you are looking for a career move rather than just a job, in which you can develop over a period of years.

Older women may find that their applications do not gain them interviews as the recruiter assumes that they may have children to look after and would therefore be less reliable as employees. Again, you must tackle this immediately, indicating that this is not so.

The points above cannot all be raised – use your discretion. If you included everything, you would be unable to adhere to the principle of brevity. However, these are factors to bear in mind despite apparent unfairness. This should be less of a problem where the advertisement carries an equal opportunities statement.

Dual employment

If you have had more than one job at the same time during your career, you should clarify the questions of the reader in advance. State which was full time and which was part time, or give some idea of the number of hours involved if both were part time positions. Often in CV's like this, it is not clear which was the 'major' employment.

Many managers also lecture on a part time basis or write publications relating to their field of work. It is useful for the recruiter to have an idea of your priorities and the level of your involvement in these additional activities. Ensure that the dates are clear and demonstrate how these extra tasks enhanced rather than detracted from your main post.

Specific fields of employment

There are often additional information items that you can add to your CV for particular types of employment.

If you are involved in sales, you will need to indicate your successes in terms of money made, reaching targets, generating profits for the company, turning losses into profits and percentages of sales.

There are generally two categories of sales specialists, those with sound technical product (or service) knowledge who are expert at that level, and those whose forte is selling, but who have proven sales ability over a range of non-technical products. It is useful to identify which category is applicable – note that advertisements for sales staff are worded to attract one category or the other. You should respond accordingly.

In advertising or public relations, you may wish to back up your application with a portfolio giving evidence of your successful campaigns. Advertising executives will quote response rates, increase in market share, ability to keep and gain more clients in a competitive field, etc. Public relations officers can quote the rising impact of whatever (or whoever) they have been promoting. Although it has been noted that recruiters usually prefer traditional CV's, if any exception is to be made, it is in the creative fields such as these.

Normally, it is not advisable to attach samples of your work (they can be your pride and joy, but can clog up the filing cabinets of others!), but designers can be an exception to this rule. Descriptions of work can be valuable but the articles themselves may have far more impact. If it is not possible to send samples, *good* photographs may be sent. Common sense is necessary here – you may have designed a car engine but it would be rather expensive and bulky to send all the plans, etc! And no, do not be tempted to drive it round...!

Computer staff vary their CV's to fit the type of work too. Whilst it is not generally good practice to list all the machines or types of work, computer analysts and programmers must quantify exactly what their experience has taught them to use. This may mean listing 'responsible for development of VAX, DEC, ...' etc. but this can be quite acceptable.

Secretarial staff too, must avoid particular pitfalls. Many young secretaries include height, weight, and colour of eyes on the CV's. If they are to be taken seriously they would keep their applications to details of their abilities rather than attempting to convince selectors that they would make good models. As mentioned earlier, discretion can be used on some skills. If an advertisement calls for shorthand, speedwriting of sufficient speed is usually acceptable. The exception is if a particular type of shorthand is prescribed. In those cases there are probably others in the office who would need to interpret it and read it back.

Managers and senior executives may choose to put in a career summary on the CV after their personal details. The reader wants to see immediately what the individual is capable of and experienced in. The career summary must therefore be carefully angled to bring out the strands of the employment history, duties and strengths relevant to the post applied for, the advertisement and the business. Past (transferable and respected) achievements must be emphasised.

Consultants should avoid saying 'freelance consultancy' on CV's. This conveys the impression that this is a cover up for unemployment. If you have been involved in consultancy, give examples of the main theme of the consultancy, a synopsis of a few particular sample assignments (with durations) and client companies. Be prepared to give full details at an interview.

Checklist

School leavers and those applying for their first jobs:

1. *Is your CV very brief? Can you reduce it further?*
2. *Have you put in qualifications with grades, clearly?*
3. *Have you noted relevant work experience (and said whether it was part time, holiday work, or work experience organised from school, etc)?*
4. *Have you used your interests to show aptitudes?*

After unemployment or redundancy

1. *Have you said something about what you have been doing since your last job? Does it sound positive and useful?*
2. *Have you managed to sound positive about your last job?*
3. *Have you angled your unsolicited applications and speculative letters to the job and the company?*

After career breaks

1. *Have you shown your commitment to the post?*
2. *Have you demonstrated transferable skills?*

3. *Have you given good reasons for the career gaps?*
4. *Have you managed to show the positive side of your overseas experience?*
5. *Are any testimonials that you have attached translated into English?*

Women

1. *Have you shown that you have good child care arrangements or will not have children yet?*
2. *Have you shown that you will not take time off work and can work extra hours occasionally?*
3. *Have you made it clear that you are seeking a career?*

Dual employment

1. *Are the dates and exact details of your posts clear?*
2. *Have you demonstrated to the employer the value of these extra jobs?*
3. *Is it clear that any extra paid work that you undertake will not interfere with the position you are applying for?*

Specific fields of employment

See notes for special requirements in particular fields of employment such as sales, advertising and public relations, design, secretarial work, management and executive positions, and consultancy.

8. Beating the opposition

'Something special'

It has already been said that with enormous competition in the labour market, it is more important than ever to have a good CV and a good application. It is not enough to show that you have the right qualifications and experience if the reader is looking at hundreds of applications for different jobs. You will need to find a way to make yours a little different, while still staying within the traditional format. The application must show a touch of flair, something a little bit special or unusual. If the recruiter is looking through many CV's, yours must not be the boring one that goes to the bottom of the pile (or worse still, into the waste paper bin!). This means that your CV must not be bland. It must be used to wake the recruiter up! An added interest or unexpected achievement can do this, or something which helps your personality shine through from the facts about you.

The 'something special' that you add to your CV must give just a taste of something to interest the reader. The object is to initiate curiosity and whet the appetite rather than giving all the details of whatever you choose. Giving all the details means that you would have less to talk about to fill in the gaps at an interview and it takes out the impact. If you give all the information, the CV can look longer whilst still being basically boring. You must give the recruiter what he or she wants to see in terms of facts and then something to entertain too.

Be seen as a nice person!

If you are putting in details of interests which are not self-centred, this will help the employer to see you as a nice person. There may be hundreds of applications and many people who seem (on paper at least) able to do the job, but the recruiter will see it as a bonus if he or she feels able to *like* you, having read your curriculum vitae. If the recruiter is taking on staff for others this not only makes the interviewing task more pleasant, but increases his credibility with the person in the company for whom he is recruiting.

Other ways to come across as a 'nice person' include not running down your present employer. The individual recruiting wants to be assured of your loyalty to the company – this will be hard if it looks as if you have been very fed up with each of your last companies and/or bosses. Nobody wants to employ someone who is going to give a bad impression of their organisation when they are thinking of leaving. As mentioned in the section on redundancy, this is important here too. It will help if you can convey the feeling that although you were disappointed for yourself at being made redundant, you can see the logic of the decisions behind this. Employers are then likely to be impressed by your ability to cope with the stress of the situation in a well-balanced and fair manner. You will seem eminently reasonable, a nice person and hopefully an ideal employee.

Allied to this is the point that personality clashes must be minimised. The reader is far more liable to be suspicious that you are difficult to work with, than to wholeheartedly embrace your views that you work with a complete tyrant. Don't forget either, that there may be complete tyrants in the new company that someone has to work with!

You should also avoid showing too much interest in salary and conditions of service at the beginning. It is acceptable for sales staff on commission terms to ask questions about this, because their potential earnings are related to their sales or the profit that they have made for the organisation. Otherwise though, keep queries on payments, the type of office furniture, number of days holiday, company discounts, etc in the background. If you want to negotiate on these, do so once the position has been offered when you know that the company wants to employ you. Whilst you must not undersell yourself, your prime interest must be seen to be the scope of the employment and the fascination of an interesting job in a good company, not how much you will take home. Avoid being seen as a money-grabber.

Avoid gushing too! Applications and letters which state that the applicant is 'good with people' or a 'jolly person to have around' irritate rather than impress readers. Aim to communicate your cheerfulness by your attitude and perhaps a touch of humour instead of stating it directly. Many people also state that they have initiative. Bland statements of this type are impossible to quantify. Do not waste words by saying this, provide evidence of it in the details you give on achievements instead. 'I have shown initiative' is guaranteed to make the recruiter want proof, and proof is an important factor here. If you really do have the initiative that the employer is seeking, make it shine through the application.

Do not try to gain the potential employer's sympathy either. If you are applying for a position that demands qualifications of a certain level and you did not gain them due to a personal tragedy, do not say that, particularly if it was a long time ago. You may know that you would have passed with flying colours but for the intimely family trauma, but however reasonable your excuse is to you, the employer will still interpret it as merely an excuse. The recruiter may also feel that you are trying to manipulate his or her feelings so that you are interviewed out of sympathy. This may seem very hard (and is) but you should make the best of this by stressing your other positive attributes.

Be positive

Aim to sound positive and confident in your CV and application. Be definite in your statements so that you say 'I am good at organising special functions' rather than 'I feel that I am good at organising some of the special functions which I have been involved with'. The former statement is much stronger and is unequivocal. Do not waffle. State clearly what you want to say in a confident manner. If you think that you lack confidence, see the section below on self analysis. It is imperative that you write your CV when you are feeling positive and can appreciate your own strengths. Never, never write your CV, application forms or covering letter when you are feeling depressed because your negative feelings will be communicated in the phrases and sentences that you use. This is particularly difficult if you are unemployed but it is very important to make the effort to lift yourself out of the negative thoughts. You must work hard to enable yourself to identify your own positive points, personal skills and abilities.

Do not waste your own time and energy (and perhaps money) applying for positions that you are very unlikely to be offered. Receiving letter after letter of rejection is demoralising and makes it much harder for you to be positive fifty applications on. If you know that you can do the job, it is up to you to provide evidence of that to convince the employer. If you 'just know' that you can do it but have nothing to back up your argument, this will be very difficult.

Do not itemise your bad points or problems that you have experienced at work. You may be asked at an interview what your weak points are, but leave these out of the CV. Your CV or application is the means by which you sell yourself – it must be effective and persuasive. Putting in things that you are not good at is counter productive, off-putting to the recruiter and wastes space which you could be using to sell your strengths and capabilities. Do not be swayed by a desire to be honest – by including only your good skills you are not denying your particular human failings but merely gearing your CV to your positive attributes. All your competitors for this employment will be doing the same, so ensure that you compete on an equal basis.

Self analysis

This is the key to a successful application. It is not easy to sum up the *key* aspects of your career in a way which interests employers. You can begin by jotting down a few basic facts about yourself and what you have done. Write down all the things you can think of at first, then analyse these carefully. Begin to be selective about which you would include in your CV, taking only those that seem directly relevant to what you did, and to future employers. Prune these down so that you have some brief but representative details. Do not say things like 'Mr. Jones, my boss, thinks that the office would not run without me'. Put in details of specific duties and responsibilities that you had, mention things that you can do and include your strengths in that. Avoid generalisations and including the opinions of others. You must show that you know your own mind and have confidence in yourself.

As mentioned earlier, CV's should never be written when you are depressed. If you have had many letters of rejection or are unemployed, it is easy to become demoralised and despairing. Also if you have been doing your current job for a long time or are very bored with it, it can be difficult to realise what your strengths are. Things that you do easily and have done for a long time tend to lose value and you forget how difficult those things may be for others to do. It is typical that people in these positions assume that 'anyone can do that' because they are so used to it. To begin to release yourself from this trap, you must start to look at your job and the tasks which you can do in the same way that an outsider would. Think about which are specific to your current position but also which would be useful to other employers. Vocational guidance may also help you to analyse and identify aptitudes that you have not already revealed (or only partly noticed) in your career so far. The advantage of this kind of thing and of the psychological testing so often associated with it is that you then have some impartial but reliable, expert evidence to back up your application. Remember that this may not be enough without additional training but it should certainly help. Use this as part of your self-selling process.

If you are really stuck and have no expert advice available to help you, think of your job in terms of the constituent skills using the same categories used in the Youth Training Scheme by the Manpower Services Commission. The scheme was designed to give young people transferable skills – think about your own in the same way. The four basic areas are communication, number, problem solving and practical. Sometimes computer literacy is added. Within these main headings, the core areas are broken down into core skills and key tasks. These include operating with numbers, recognising cost and value, working with people, planning practical activities, diagnosing problems, preparing for practical activities, etc. The key words include count, measure, diagnose, check, correct, etc. This is a useful concept to allow you to break down your own abilities to transferable skills. It enables you to make the link between your experience or hobbies and your abilities. An example would be organising an amateur theatre production. This could include the ability to plan (timetabling and assessing priorities), arranging advertising, preparation of simple budgets, obtaining necessary props (ensuring adequate preparation and showing an ability to think ahead) and organising the box office. The latter may entail looking after the finances as well as persuading someone to collect the tickets, etc. In addition to the points noted, this kind of activity also shows that the individual can work as part of a team and implies good communication skills.

This exercise is also useful if you are unemployed. You can think about any previous experience that you have and may be able to utilise spare time interests too. More active leisure pursuits may also give useful pointers; a good snooker player may have a very accurate eye and make a good proof reader, or a long distance runner may demonstrate the tenacity which he or she also uses in research skills.

If you are unemployed and are applying for a job which you feel is below the level of the one you did previously, you may need to minimise your achievements to some extent (not too much if there would be good promotion prospects).

You may wish to cite a need to regain the quality of your life, a useful euphemism covering desire to avoid commuting, getting home at a reasonable time, not having to change location, or finding a greener, more pleasant working environment. You must show this as a positive decision and emphasise through your application that it does not represent an inability to cope with constant pressure, but a disillusionment with the 'rat race' in general. Retain the impression that you are willing and able to work hard.

Angling the application to fit the job

The whole thrust of this book has been to help you edit and amplify your background and experience to fit the post that you intend to apply for. You must do this without misrepresenting yourself, but by angling the CV or application to the job. That means pulling out of your background the threads which show continuity. All good CV's show a logical progression from one post to another. The art is in persuading the reader that the progression is logical and planned, even if you know it was not quite that easy!

If your application is unsolicited, you will have to work even harder to make it match the kind of position you are looking for, in the type of organisation you are applying to.

Select key tasks in each of your past posts and include only the ones which have not been improved upon by a later job. Keep in those which indicate a different dimension. This pattern can also be followed for qualifications. For instance, if a secretary has RSA shorthand qualifications at 70, 80 and 90 words per minute, it is only necessary to quote the 90 wpm, particularly if they were taken together as is often the case. In the work context, this can be seen in the following example. An individual has assisted in planning estimates and budgetary control in one position but has then taken sole charge of this after a promotion. In that case, there may be other aspects of the job not done after the promotion but which would be useful to highlight, eg:

Job 1:
Task 1 – assisting in planning estimates and budgetary control
Task 2 – dealing with all customer complaints
Task 3 – 8 ...

Job 2:
Task 1 – responsibility for accuracy of all estimates and budgets
Tasks 2 – 8 ... etc.

In the first job, task one could be omitted, but task two is not covered in the second job so would be left in to add a different dimension. Naturally the tasks would not be listed in this manner, but the example is a useful demonstration of the principle.

Practise not waffling. You must develop the ability to put across points succinctly but not abruptly. Continue to revise and develop the CV, constantly fine tuning the wording.

In addition to facts about your background, your CV or application form and covering letter can be used to indicate loyalty to your employers, reliability, helpfulness and honesty, cheerfulness, enough intelligence to undertake the duties set (but not too much) and a willingness to work hard without complaining. It is impossible to give a formula for a CV which will cover all these factors as well as the basics expected, but if your words are chosen carefully, the right attitude can be demonstrated. Remember that the material you include in your CV will probably form the basis of your interview and you should have an opportunity to amplify these points at that stage.

If you lack the qualifications requested in the advertisement but decide to apply anyway, do not gloss over this or ignore it. You may be sure that the recruiter will notice. You must explain the situation in as favourable a way as possible so that you improve your chances of being considered. If you would be eligible to take the qualification which you currently lack, indicate a willingness to do so if this is appropriate. This helps to show that you are keen and that you want to develop yourself. If the advertisement requires a professional qualification which you would be prepared to study for, do some research first. Do not just indicate your willingness but show it too by saying where you would take it and on what basis the course is run, eg 'I would be happy to supplement my qualifications by taking the course in x. This is available at my local college as an evening course'. Even if you hope that the employer would give you time off to study and pay for the course, do not make a big issue of this. Indicate that you have thought about it but do not pursue it too enthusiastically until the post is offered to you.

If you are able to gain any information on the promotion patterns of the potential employer, this can be helpful. Tailor your application or CV to that and say that you hope to progress in x years or months towards whatever is the next logical step in that organisation. Make sure that what you say will fit the employer's expectations. Do check the attitudes here if you can – if the employer is unable to offer promotion prospects, the payment may compensate, but no recruiter will want to think that you will be using the post purely as a stepping stone to better things. If you are unable to find out anything about prospects before an interview, do not mention it in your application. You will be able to explore the possibilities at an interview later. If you give the impression that you are so dynamic that you expect to be doing the job of the person you are applying to in six months time, an interview may not be forthcoming!

Look at the actual words you have chosen in your CV or application. Make sure that they reflect what you want to say. Earlier in this section an example was used where the task was to 'assist' in estimates and budgetary control. Many recruiters are suspicious of this word as it gives no idea of what the applicant is actually doing. 'Assist' can mean anything from undertaking the whole process in the name of someone else who got the credit, or can mean supplying the most menial piece of information to add to the estimate.

You should be specific about the type of help given and the level and duration of the responsibilities. If you are used to running the office in the absence of your boss, say what kind of office it is and how often your boss was absent. Do not exaggerate; truth may emerge later from the references.

Avoid using jargon in your application or CV. If the employer is unable to understand what you are trying to say, it will be assumed that your communication skills are poor. If you are likely to suffer from an excess of jargon, ask a friend who is not involved in the business to check the wording for you. Ensure that he or she can understand it. If you have to explain, change the CV so that it is understandable. It is very easy to slip into the jargon and use 'buzzwords' specific to your industry, forgetting that they can be misunderstood by others. If in doubt, leave it out!

The computer industry abounds with jargon. You should indicate that you understand this, without falling into the trap of being swamped in buzzwords that will impress nobody.

Checklist

1. *Have you found that 'something special' to put into your CV?*
2. *Is your CV or application boring? If so, why? (Try again!)*
3. *Do you seem to be a nice person, from the application or CV?*
4. *Do you sound positive?*
5. *Have you analysed what you want?*
6. *Have you analysed your transferable skills?*
7. *Have you edited or amplified your experience to show your best points for this job?*
8. *Have you made the link between your experience and the requirements of the post?*
9. *Have you shown that your lack of qualifications is not important or that you can make up for this by other strengths.*
10. *Have you checked the employer's promotion patterns?*
11. *Have you chosen your words with care? They should convey precise meanings.*
12. *Have you avoided using jargon and catchphrases?*

9. Letters of introduction

Letters of introduction fall into several different categories, each of which is dealt with in this chapter. Naturally there are basic skills of letterwriting and there is a basic etiquette which should be adhered to. However, within this format there is the possibility of flexibility.

Letters confirming acceptability of the interview date have not been dealt with here. These can be very simple and you should merely follow the guidelines given in the section on basic letterwriting. If you are unable to attend the interview on the date shown, or at that time, you should telephone the company first to see if this can be rearranged, then write to confirm all the details. Avoid changing the arrangements if at all possible though, as the recruiter will normally have a fairly tight schedule to follow and will want to see all the interviewees for the post in the same day or week, so that a decision can be made quickly.

You should always send a covering letter with curriculum vitae and application forms. If your letter and application is unsolicited and speculative, this is even more important. Note the comments in the section on special cases (special notes for the unemployed and school leavers etc) when you write the letter. Ensure that you do not merely repeat the information in the CV or application form – if you cannot think of anything different to say, at least make sure that you use different words to convey the same message!

The reason for sending a letter is to ensure that all the facts are in front of the prospective employer. Telephone messages necessarily screen out a large amount of the information which you may wish to convey and you have no control over which parts are related back and which parts are forgotten. In addition, the emphasis can be changed entirely.

Analyse and decide what you *want*. Make sure that the total effect of your application, CV and letter tells the reader this.

When composing speculative letters, it is all too easy to put in a good CV and letter stating why your experience etc. is relevant, but *without* stating what you want and expect.

In the same way as in CV's and application forms, do not waffle. Saying that 'Mr. Saunders, my boss, says that the office would not run without me' tells the reader nothing except that you value Mr. Saunders' opinion! Keep to the facts, make sure that they are succinct and that you say what you actually did in a positive but concise manner.

Avoid any reference to 'personal reasons' in letters (and CV's or application forms too). These *always* make the reader more curious to know the details.

Always send your letters and applications etc. by first class post and make sure that you have copies. Many people keep copies of their curriculum vitae but forget to take a copy of the covering letter. This can be very awkward if you are called for interview a long time after you wrote the letter as it is difficult to remember exactly what you said.

The basics of letterwriting

Ensure that you choose a good quality paper, ideally in A4 size so that it fits well with any other supporting documentation that you will be sending. Do not use highly coloured paper or paper with designs on it – most recruiters find this unbelievably twee and resent it intensely. Most employers prefer A4 size, as foolscap and quarto will not fit in with the other items in their filing cabinets and will either get lost or will become very tatty as part of the paper overhangs beyond the 'normal' size. The same principle that applies to CV's and application forms also applies with letters, in that you should endeavour to fold these as little as possible.

Your letter can be typed or handwritten as long as the end result is clear. The letter must be neat – many applications have been turned down because the recruiter was unable to read the contents, or the overall effect of the application showed that no effort had been put into it at all. If you choose to write the letter by hand, your writing must be legible. In most cases it is better to type the letter unless the advertiser specifically asks for handwritten ones. Where this is requested, the recruiter may be using graphology techniques to analyse your response. Have a look at a book on the subject and find out in advance what your handwriting is saying about you. You may want to modify a characteristic or so before responding! Graphological analysis is still comparatively rare in this country though, so your main aim must be to keep it neat and legible.

Use black ink for writing or typing your letter as this may well be photocopied along with your CV or application form, particularly if you have said something useful in it.

The usual rules of spelling and grammar apply equally in letters as in CV's and application forms. It is not enough to find a friend to check your beautifully presented and designed CV without asking them to check the covering letter too. This will be read before the CV because its purpose is to introduce that and it is therefore the letter that makes the very first impact.

Any letter that you send in connection with gaining employment must be formal. It must be set out properly and show respect to the person you are writing to. Remember that if you start the letter by saying 'Dear Sir' you must end with 'Yours faithfully' and that if you use the person's name as in 'Dear Mr. Gardener' you should end with 'Yours sincerely'. Note that both the 'f' of faithfully and the 's' of sincerely are in lower case script and should not be given capital letters.

Do not address letters to 'Dear Madame' – in English, there is no 'e' on the end, this is either a French spelling or insulting! The old rules on letterwriting were that you should avoid 'Dear Sir or Madam' too, on the grounds that if you did not know the sex of the recipient, you should automatically assume that it would be male. This is disappearing now though and there are no hard and fast rules.

Note how the title of the recipient is given in the advertisement. If the text asks you to reply to Mr. D. Jackson, write back saying 'Dear Mr. Jackson', do not put his initial in here, only use it in the address. If the advertisement asks for responses to David Smith, make sure that you do not write back to 'Dear David', but keep formal and address him as 'Mr. Smith'. Many people find themselves irritated by assumed familiarity from people they do not even know. If you are not responding to an advertisement, make sure that the employer is addressed in a formal manner.

Put your address in the top right hand corner of the letter (you should not technically put in your name here although many people do). If you put in the name and address of the recipient, this should be further down the page on the left-hand side. Depending on your style of letter, the date can go either beneath your own address or beneath that of the person you are writing to.

Space your letter out as well as you can so that this and the CV are both clear and neatly presented. If the letter is short, such as one merely requesting an application form you will have to begin it further down the page and give a larger space for the signature. If you have quite a lot of information to convey, such as in an unsolicited application or to highlight relevant parts of a curriculum vitae, this should start higher up the page and give less space for the signature. It is no longer necessary to stick to absolute guidelines on the spacing but you must endeavour to ensure that the overall effect is pleasing.

An example of a well set out letter requesting an application form is shown on page 84.

You will see in the letter that Miss White has asked Hanwex to send the form 'shortly'. This is fine on this kind of letter, when both parties want to act quickly, but you should use 'in due course' or some similar phrase when returning the application form so that the employer does not feel that you are attempting to hurry him up!

```
                                    46 Bluebell Rise
                                    New Horton
                                    Wiltshire
                                    SN33 4JF


Mr Alex Black
Personnel Officer
Hanwex Toy Shops
11-17 Brook Street
Swindon
Wiltshire
SN2 2XX                             12 October 1988


Dear Mr Black

                    REF: LT/126

I noticed your advertisement in the
Leisure Today journal for an Accounts
Supervisor.  I would be very grateful if
you would send me an application form for
this.

I look forward to hearing from you shortly.

Yours sincerely


Josephine White (Miss)
```

In the example shown above Miss White has used her title on the covering letter too. If she had used initials only, such as J. White, the employer would have responded to 'Mr. White' as it is always assumed that women include their titles. If your name is self explanatory or you do not want to give your title though, this is not strictly necessary.

Letters with application forms

The example above shows how you should write a letter requesting an application form. The example on the opposite page shows how you should write a letter which accompanies the application form when you return it. This, again, should be very short. Most of the information you want the employer to see will be on the application form itself, but it is polite to send a covering letter rather than send only the form. The principles outlined in the section above still apply and the letter should be very simple.

```
                              89 High Street
                              Foxton
                              Edinburgh
                              EH56 2KK


                              25 April 1984


Dear Mr Pickford

I would like to apply for the post of
Sales Administrator which was advertised
recently in the Edinburgh Post.

I have read the job description with
great interest and enclose my completed
application form.

I look forward to hearing from you.

Yours sincerely



Jane Haslett (Mrs)
```

Note that the letter does not say that Mrs. Haslett looks forward to seeing Mr. Pickford at an interview. This is a common mistake and many employers find it presumptuous. Mrs. Haslett should have enough confidence in her application without having to say that and needs only to say that she looks forward to hearing from the company. Remember too, that the first communication from the employer may not be an invitation to an interview, or a letter of rejection immediately, but many companies acknowledge each application. They are then free to wait until they have collected all the responses they expect and assess each at that stage.

Letters to send with CV's

You should always send a covering letter with your curriculum vitae. The purpose of the CV is to give details of your background and experience. You will have learnt to slant this towards the type of post you are seeking and the organisation, but the letter is needed so that you can state exactly what you want. The letter should give the reference shown in the advertisement if there is one and state which post you are applying for. This is especially important if the advertisement mentions more than one vacancy, but should be done anyway. A letter which does not state this looks sloppy.

Ensure before you start writing that you will be sending the letter to the right person, using the correct address and postcode and quoting the right department within the company. Failure to do this can mean that the application is delayed and may not arrive before the closing date.

Spend some time composing your letter and avoid clichés. As noted earlier, the letter is important as this will be read before the CV itself. It therefore creates the first impression and sets the tone of the application. Always compose the letter as a rough draft first before you write out the one you intend to send. Write the kind of letter you would like to read yourself. It should, like the CV, be factual but interesting. It must contain all the salient points not included in the CV but which are pertinent to this particular application. You may wish to draw attention to particular factors within the CV which apply to the post you are interested in.

You should avoid using phrases such as 'I can communicate effectively at all levels'. This, like the phrase 'I have initiative…' is virtually impossible to prove without added detail which takes up space. If you have initiative, or can communicate effectively at all levels, make sure that this is evident from the information in your CV. Restating it will not help – if it is obvious from other details, the recruiter will notice it.

You should avoid using phrases such as these if the advertisement asks for these kinds of qualities. Other applicants will doubtless be stating that they have great initiative or whatever in their applications too and that would mean that your application would look exactly like all the others.

Two examples of covering letter are shown overleaf. In the first, imagine that Mr. Smithson is applying to Matrix Engines Ltd. whose specialisms are engines for light aircraft (mostly pleasure planes which make trips around the Norfolk cost for holidays in Great Yarmouth) and ocean going yachts but are now beginning to develop their speedboat engines. They are a small but expanding company, which has just gone public.

Mr. Smithson has a lot of experience in marketing, which was mainly in the aviation industry (for an international airline) but also worked for a company called Speedsure in the past which sold speedboats. Speedsure will now be one of Matrix Engines' competitors; they may know of the advertising campaign which Mr. Smithson conducted for them. Mr. Smithson naturally thinks that he would be ideal for the post of Marketing Manager which has been advertised locally.

Note that Mr. Smithson's reference to his home town shows the prospective employer that he would not have to relocate to take up this post and Mr. Smithson has highlighted the past experience he has which would be relevant to Matrix Engines.

6 Seaview House
20 Exmouth Street
Great Yarmouth
Norfolk NR4 7DL

Mr P Baker
Personnel Department
Matrix Engines Ltd
Worsthorpe Estate
Great Yearmouth
Norfolk NR1 9RT   17 March 1985

Dear Mr Baker

Advertisement Reference: NE/132

I would like to apply for the position of
Marketing Manager which was advertised in
the Norwich Echo on Wednesday.

As you will see from my enclosed CV, I
have been employed in the marketing field
for ten years and have been particularly
involved with promotions and market
research for the aviation industry. In
addition my work with Speedsure Ltd
enabled me to take total responsibility
for the successful advertising campaign
which increased the percentage of market
share by a third for their speedboats.

I would be very interested in the
possibility of working with your company
to expand its market and prestige within
my home town.

I look forward to hearing from you.

Yours sincerely

M K Smithson

32 Bury Lane
Manchester
M90 8SU

Ms J Hope
Editor
The New Electronics
P X Publishing Ltd
PX House
Salford Road
Salford M87 5TQ   1 June 1986

Dear Ms Hope

I would like to apply for the position of
Editorial Assistant advertised in the
Guardian yesterday.

As you will see from my Curriculum Vitae
I have had a scientific background coupled
with experience in publishing. I have
designed many advertisements for clients
which have been used in lengthy campaigns
(examples of these can be supplied). I
am used to working to deadlines, liaising
with printers and have developed an eye
for detail from helping the production
department of my company during a two
month spell last year.

I have a good general education and
specialised in electronics as part of my
physics degree course. I am determined
to prove my ability to write effectively
by hard work and natural flair!

I would appreciate your consideration for
this post and look forward to hearing
from you in the near future.

Yours sincerely

William Johns

In the second example, on page 89, William Johns is applying for a post with a company which publishes many scientific magazines and journals. He has been involved in the publishing business before but has been selling advertising space rather than employed in the editorial sections. He has had experience of designing advertisements though, and brings this point out in his covering letter. His current post was his first since leaving university and he recognises that the editorial world is particularly difficult to break into.

William Johns has tried to be persuasive but not 'pushy' here and realises that it needs determination to be noticed. He has indicated that he is willing to provide evidence of his achievements but has not overloaded the employer with paper at this stage. This is important. Examples of work should not be sent with the initial application but you should rely on saying enough in the curriculum vitae and covering letter to interest the reader. Be prepared to provide supplementary evidence of this nature if requested though. You may be asked to send it or bring it to an interview. If you have published works which could be found easily, assume that the employer will look these up if interested. If the items are not so readily accessible, have copies ready to send. You should provide a representative sample of your work. The person who reads your application first may be in the personnel section. If the recruiter receives a huge stack of photocopies he or she may not necessarily pass these on to the section of the company where you wish to be employed, and where they would understand the material. Sending massive tomes also increases the chances of having the whole application thrown away.

Letters to consultants

When writing to consultants, follow the normal rules of basic letterwriting, but be much more specific about what you want if you are not responding to an advertisement for a particular vacancy. You may need to give the consultant more information so that he or she can suggest vacancies which you may be interested in applying for. You should tell the consultant what salary you are seeking (or give a range, or a minimum if that is easier) and you should also give details of any companies which you do not want to work for, so that your curriculum vitae and details will not be sent on by an enthusiastic consultant before you have had a chance to stop it.

You must convince the consultant that you are good in your chosen career. Your application to the consultant must look professional; then it will be easier for him or her to see that you will be relatively easy to place in a job. If the consultant is convinced, your case will be carried with more conviction to the client company.

Speculative letters

These are letters to companies, enquiring about the possibility of employment where they have not advertised a particular vacancy. The idea is to attract their attention before the post is advertised. If the company knows that a post will be vacant soon (through retirement of the present encumbent, or if they always take on trainees at a set time in the year, for instance), you may be considered before the position is advertised. In some cases you could save them the cost of advertising.

You must be sure that you tell the prospective employer what you are looking for in terms of employment (but not salary). The object is to describe yourself in a positive, memorable manner. The company may have no posts vacant when you write in, but your objective is that they consider you for future positions.

You must use the letter and CV in the same way as you would for an advertised job. Find out the name and title of the appropriate person to write to, and address him or her by name. You know what you want and should still make an effort to angle your application to the sort of job you want in that kind of organisation. Look at the background of the firm, its size and location. Make sure that you know what its main business is and also what subsidiaries it has, if applicable. Find details of its recent history and whether it is expanding or stable. (If it is contracting, you may choose not to apply there!)

Unsolicited letters should not be much longer than those responding to advertisements. Keep your sentences short. If you divide your letter into four paragraphs, the first would be an introduction saying that you are enquiring about employment with the company. If you have been referred to them by someone impressive, you can say so here, but it should be someone who will not pressurise the organisation (i.e. not a competitor) and it must be someone worth quoting, otherwise leave it out.

Use the second paragraph to give salient details of your own skills and strengths – this can be very brief as your curriculum vitae will give most of the details. In the third paragraph, make the link between your own skills and any of the company's requirements that you have identified. Show how you satisfy the requirements that you have isolated, but emphasise just a couple of the points which you think will interest them.

The last paragraph would merely say that you can supply further information if this would be helpful and that you look forward to hearing from them. Executives may also add that they would welcome the opportunity to have a brief discussion on this. You should avoid putting pressure on, as it will only make the reader annoyed.

You may wish to follow up a speculative letter by a telephone call. Again, do not pressurise the recipient – if he or she has not already read your letter and CV, any pressure will make this even less likely. You should be polite but direct, ask clear questions and do not waffle. Think of any questions which you are likely to be asked before you ring, so that your answers can be prepared and will show you in the best light possible.

If you are nervous about telephoning, but still want to do it, use assertiveness techniques to help you. Make sure that you telephone from a place where you will not be disturbed, plan what you are going to say and stand up while you make the call. This sounds silly until you try it but has the psychological benefit of making you feel more powerful, especially if you know that the person you are calling will be sitting down. Try not to be put off – ask whether it would be convenient for them to see you soon or whether you may call back in two weeks or a month or whatever. You must avoid being seen as a nuisance, but without giving them an opportunity to say no. If you just ask whether you can see them, or suggest a specific time and date, it will be a lot easier for them to refuse you.

An example of a speculative letter is shown overleaf. In the letter you will see that Mrs. Hunter has taken on board the principles outlined above, but has also made her commitment to working clear. The employer should be happy to accept that she realises that extra work would be required at times and that her young family will not prevent her from helping out on these occasions. She has offered to send references from a previous employer early on (to show that she is a good worker) and the fact that she has stayed in contact with him makes her sound a likeable and loyal person.

In this example, the applicant has said very little about the demands and successes of the job – as a legal secretary she would obviously have many responsibilities, but would take mainly a supporting role, about which less can be said. The curriculum vitae she would have attached would have given details of her secretarial qualifications and she has mentioned a refresher course which she used to update her knowledge and skills.

6 Long Lane
Thorpesbury
Near York
York   YO3 3WZ

Mr Charles Bradford
Personnel Manager
J Braithwaite & Co
Cathedral Street
York   YO2 9CN   25 November 1989

Mr Bradford

I have just moved into the York area and
am interested in finding employment as a
legal secretary here.

I worked for five years in this capacity
for a large practice of solicitors before
having a career break to bring up my young
family. In order to keep updated, I have
just finished a refresher course at my
local college.

I understand that your main business is in
the conveyancing field; my main experience
is also in this area. I can provide
references from my previous employer (with
whom I have stayed in contact) and am
interested in progressing my career through
hard work with your firm. I know the
problems (but also the challenge and
rewards) of working late to finalise last
minute details for clients and would be
happy to do this again!

I would appreciate the opportunity to
discuss this with you and look forward
to hearing from you.

Yours sincerely

Claire Hunter (Mrs)

Checklist

1. *Have you used A4 paper and black ink or typescript?*
2. *Is the name and address of the recipient clear and correct?*
3. *Have you told the reader what you want?*
4. *Have you made sure that the beginning and ending are correct for each other (eg, 'Yours faithfully' with 'Dear Sir' and 'Yours sincerely' with 'Dear Ms. X')?*
5. *Is the letter neat and well spaced?*
6. *Have you checked the letter for errors in spelling and grammar? Has this been double-checked for you?*
7. *Have you quoted the advertisement reference?*
8. *Does the letter give all the relevant facts without waffling?*
9. *Have you avoided repeating chunks of the curriculum vitae or application form?*
10. *Have you made the link between your experience and the requirements of the employer?*
11. *Have you avoided clichés and irritating catchphrases?*
12. *Have you told consultants what salary you are seeking and which companies you are not interested in working for?*

10. Application forms

If you have applied for a job and been sent an application form to complete, the first thing to do is photocopy it so that you can fill in the draft rather than making mistakes on the original document. Never write straight on to an application form without doing this and planning it first.

Application forms can be handwritten or typed. Use your discretion – it can sometimes be difficult to fit typing into the spaces unless you are used to this. If you write the form by hand, make sure that your writing is clear and neat and use black ink. Write the form in capital letters as it makes it easier for the recipient to read. Use a ruler to make sure that your writing stays in a straight horizontal line. Forms covered in neat writing that rises (or falls) towards the right hand side of the page look messy.

Send the application form with a brief covering letter. This need only say that you are enclosing the application form for the post of x advertised in y newspaper. If you have already sent a letter to request the form, this may also be kept and be clipped to the returned form. It is therefore useful to ensure that all your responses to advertisements are on similar paper so that the overall effect is consistent.

If you have been sent an application form but have already sent a full CV and covering letter to the organisation, you may find this very irritating. However, if you want the job, you must comply. Fill in the form carefully – do not assume that the company will have kept your CV, and make sure that you highlight all the pertinent facts again.

The application form is important as it is often the basis of the contract of employment with the organisation once you have been offered the job. Mistakes or falsehoods on this can invalidate the contract.

Address the whole process in the same way as if you had just read the advertisement and were designing a new CV.

Look at the advertisement and analyse it for requirements and inferences. Analyse your own experience, good points and background in general. Take time to compose the answers to the questions, ensure that they give a fair illustration of you and that you have shown (as nearly as possible) a logical career progression. Note the qualities you possess which are particularly apt for each application.

If the advertiser has sent company literature and a detailed job description with the application form, ensure that you read this thoroughly before you begin to compose your answers on the form. This will supplement the information that you were given in the advertisement and will probably provide extra specific details. A good job description will include not only a list of the main duties in the job, but also specific tasks and a hierarchy chart. If the latter is not included there may well be references to the person you would be responsible to and any subordinates who would be responsible to you (with numbers of staff and the size of the department).

Some job descriptions also contain information on the salary scales, the grade of the job, the qualifications needed and the working conditions, and details of holiday entitlements etc. Liaison with other people can be included as well. The liaison section is sometimes broken down into liaison with other individuals in the organisation and that with people and bodies outside. Another way of subdividing this information is used by some organisations, that is to split this section into liaison with superiors, liaison with peers and liaison with subordinates. Lines of responsibility can also be given including formal lines (that is, who you would be directly answerable to) and informal lines (perhaps a functional supervisor who sets your work, although strictly speaking you would be responsible to someone else). This kind of informal chain of command is quite common in situations where teams of people work together on projects, perhaps for a limited duration.

The advantage of an application form to the recruiter is that the facts will appear in just the place he or she expects. If you think that this does not enable you to present yourself in the best light possible, you can attach a copy of your own CV to the application form. However, you should have become quite experienced at picking the salient factors from your past and adapting them to fit the application you are interested in.

You may find that the same application form is used to cover many different sorts of jobs within the firm. If this is so, do not be surprised if you cannot fill in every section in depth. The qualifications part, for instance, may be large enough to encompass the academic achievements of the specialist and technical staff and the employment history section may be large (or may ask the respondent to continue on a separate sheet if necessary) so that it could be used by the older and more senior people within the organisation. You should just ensure that the information you give will be enough for the post that you are applying for. You will already have analysed this so you should not worry further.

Application forms at interview

It is worth noting that if you respond to an advertisement by sending in a CV and covering letter, but are then invited to an interview, the company may want you to fill in their standard application form there. This means that you will have to be able to remember the details if you are not prepared. If you can, take a copy of your curriculum vitae with you to interviews as a matter of course. You will then have a document that you trust which you can refer to. Your application form will be consistent with the CV that you have already provided and the employer will be satisfied. If you make a mistake, or put down information incorrectly because you cannot remember, the employer may doubt your honesty. If that does not happen, you may still encounter problems as the application form is usually the basis of the employment contract, as noted earlier.

Content of application forms

Most application forms will say 'CONFIDENTIAL' on the top, so you should put in *all* the relevant information.

The application form will ask you for your name and address. If it asks for your full name, but you are not called by your first name, make this clear by underlining the name you are known by. You can also use that name on your covering letter, perhaps using your first initial too, eg, E. <u>Sarah</u> Golding rather than just 'Sarah'. The form may also ask you to put in your present address with a section for permanent address, if that is different. This is useful for those still studying and living away from home. If you are tempted to put in your home address and then letters inviting you to an interview are sent there, if they are not forwarded quickly the delay could cause irreparable damage.

The application form will usually ask for a telephone number too – if you cannot be contacted at work or it would be embarrassing if you were, say so.

The application form will have a space for you to give details of the post applied for and reference number. Make sure that this is filled in correctly.

Other items in the personal section of the application form can include date of birth (make sure you do not fill in the year in which you are applying instead of the one you were born in), age, sex, marital status, number and ages of dependent children, nationality (you should not be asked for both your nationality now and your nationality at birth), years of UK residence and place of birth. The latter should show the town with the county if the town is not well known, it does not mean to ask you for the name of the hospital that you were born in. Some application forms only ask you to indicate marital status in terms of single, married or widowed. If you are separated or divorced and wish to indicate this (which can be useful if you are about to change your name), tick the 'single' box, but write 'separated' or 'divorced' beneath it.

Most application forms then go on to give you space to insert details of your qualifications and education. Use the same principles as those outlined in the section on CV's. In some forms, this section can also be used to encompass details of short courses attended, apprenticeships and professional qualifications. Most forms require the date of passing and the name of the institution where you undertook training. Many also ask for the grades you achieved in the examinations. If the grading has changed since you took them, indicate this.

In the section on qualifications, you will not be able to list those most important first as you will need to adhere to the requirements of the form. This means that if you are applying for a post but do not have all the qualifications requested in the advertisement, it will be very obvious.

Most application forms then follow with career history, sometimes with a separate preceding section on present employment. These ask you for details of your main duties and responsibilities, with the title of the post and the name and nature of business of the employer. In most cases they also ask you for salary (sometimes salary on leaving) and reasons for leaving. These aspects need careful consideration. The information given on your major responsibilities should be prepared in the same way as the compilation of your CV.

Salary information

Give details of your salary in each of your past posts where you can still remember it! This should include basic salary and commission or bonus payments (you can itemise these separately if you want to and if there is room on the form). If you have added the constituent parts of your payment package together, say so, or the employer may assume that all the money quoted is basic salary and they cannot afford to employ you.

Do not be tempted to exaggerate your current salary too much, as this may be checked with your present employer. If you do not want to give details of your salary, bear in mind that this will irritate the reader. You may wish to leave this section blank if you have previously earned more than this post commands. If the advertisement does not state the salary and you refuse to put this on your application form, you may arrive at an interview to find that the payments are too little and you could not accept. This wastes both your own and the interviewer's time.

Reasons for leaving

Be careful when filling in this section. You will probably have to justify your reasons. You must convince the potential employer that you are a sound prospect for his or her company.

Never criticise your present employer – the reader of your application form may assume that you will do that to them a few years on. Be as frank as you can about your reasons for leaving (or wanting to leave), but do not be negative. Most reasons for leaving, whilst seeming negative, can be put across in a positive way.

If you are leaving or have left a company for more money, it may be unwise to state this directly. This is especially true of those whose earnings are related to their performance in some way. Whilst most people recognise that leaving for more money can be quite legitimate, few admit it openly. You may want to ally this point to promotion prospects or just say that there was no possibility of progression in that company. If you are saying this though, you must ensure that there are prospects for advancement with the organisation you are applying to because it will be assumed that you are referring to promotion prospects. If you are in a field where it is known that your employer pays very badly, it may be easier to say this. If you are working for a charity for instance, it will be readily accepted that you would expect to earn more elsewhere.

If you are leaving because of boredom, do not say so directly. You may allude to lack of work or challenge (but usually only when you have been in the job for a while). Note that if you quote lack of challenge, the post you are applying for must be obviously more demanding on that score. If you are bored because you have been doing the job for a long time, say that you have outgrown it. Sound as if you are enthusiastic about learning new tasks, rather than just bored with the old ones. If you intend to say that you have outgrown the job, you may raise questions in the reader's mind if you are employed in a large company and would normally expect to progress within it. If you have been studying on a part time basis and the course is now complete, you can legitimately say that you have outgrown the job and that you are seeking new challenges. In that case, it is easier to show that your lack of progression is due to company structure rather than your own failing.

Avoid saying that you are overworked in your current post, even if you passionately believe this. It will give the impression that you are lazy or afraid of hard work. If you are in a supervisory or managerial position it will cast doubts on your ability to delegate and manage your own time.

If you changed your career for something entirely different, say what prompted this and whether it was the result of lengthy deliberation or if it was just an opportunity which arose but could not be missed. Despite the fact that most people aim to plan their careers, few discount the influence of luck and 'being in the right place at the right time'. Of course you would not use the latter argument alone as you would aim to persuade the reader that you were noticed for your particular skills and aptitudes.

If you have been made redundant, most recruiters will sympathise. If your unemployment is not explained – you appear from the application to have left a perfectly good job of your own accord with nothing to go to – this will arouse questions. If you have been sacked, avoid saying so directly, but explain honestly if you were unsuited to the job.

If a previous employment was terminated due to the liquidation of the business, this is acceptable. If it happens too often, though, or if you were involved at a senior level at the time, it may not go down so well.

If you have left employment due to the relocation of your partner's job, be careful how you communicate this. Your aim must be to appear a loyal and stable spouse, whilst leaving no doubt that you would be committed to the employer you are applying to. The recruiter must not be allowed to think that if your partner was moved again in a month's time, you would be taken away from the post you have just been expensively recruited to.

Never state that 'personal reasons' caused you to leave a post. This *always* arouses the curiosity of the reader but leaves him or her without any real information, just the feeling that you are secretive (the form says the information is confidential, remember). Whilst very sad, the death of a member of the family or similar is not a good reason to give. If you say 'personal reasons' on the application form, but then admit this at an interview, it will just embarrass the interviewer.

Avoid mentioning personality clashes as a reason for leaving. This makes you appear difficult to work with. Similarly, you must avoid saying that your boss or colleagues are fools – this does not do you any good and makes you sound very arrogant. Also to be avoided are comments to the effect that your boss does not know his or her job, but it may be permissible to say that you have a new boss and find it very difficult to train him or her as well as doing your own job and trying to progress. If you do this, however, you must be prepared to answer questions on why you were not promoted into that position.

Your reasons for leaving should be consistent and convincing. If you have moved employment every six months for the last three years in what is normally a very stable industry, the employer will wonder why and if you are ever going to settle. (Their first thoughts will probably be that you were sacked.)

Note that it is not sufficient to state that you left one position to take up another. Promotion is an acceptable reason, but if you have changed firms, you should state what made you decide to seek other work.

Lack of job security is a quite acceptable reason for leaving, as is the relocation of your present company. If you are going to say that your employer is not keeping updated with the market, or the particular part of it with which you are involved, you must be careful how you put this. Avoid criticising your current employer, by glossing over this so that your enthusiasm rather than their lack of business acumen comes across.

If you are planning to leave because your job interferes with your social life, do not say so! Find other, more positive ways of putting this over.

If you have been passed over for promotion, do not mention this. You may allude to lack of current prospects but be careful that you do not sound negative about your current employer. Your disillusionment may transmit itself very easily.

Health

Many application forms ask for various details about the state of your health. The questions range from simple ones asking if you are in good health and, if not, to specify. Others ask for details of previous serious illnesses and operations, number of days absent from work during the last year and whether you are registered disabled. If you answer 'yes' to the latter, further details such as date and particulars of registration can be requested.

You should be truthful about any past illnesses or disability, but describe this in a way that shows what you are capable of rather than any difficulties that you encounter in your career. Organisations employing more than twenty people should have 3 per cent disabled, so may encourage your application. If you have difficulties in getting up and down stairs, it would be wise to point this out though, as you may find that working at that company would be too awkward.

Leisure interests

Use the same criteria for selecting these as in your curriculum vitae. If a large space is allotted, put in more detail than normal, but otherwise be guided by all the factors previously mentioned. Remember to differentiate between the skills you have and your leisure interests, about which you are enthusiastic rather than good!

References

Most application forms ask for names and addresses of referees. You should use your last employer and the one before if possible. If you are not likely to get a good reference from a previous employer and you have another who you could use instead, do so. Always ensure that you know what the referees will say about you and ask their permission before quoting them.

Many employers do not take up references, despite asking for names and addresses. Others take them up purely to confirm the facts of the application, once you have been offered employment with them. Some intend to take up references so that they may be seen by the interviewing panel. If you do not want your referees to be approached, say that they should not be contacted without asking you first. This is acceptable, as recruiters recognise that most people do not want their present employers to know that they are seeking other employment.

It is difficult to estimate the importance of references realistically because most referees give glowing references and these are seldom believed anyway! Bad references would be treated with a great deal of caution though.

If you have not yet been employed, you should use academic referees – teachers or tutors who have known you well for some time. If the application requests it, you may give a personal reference (rather like a character witness), but otherwise avoid it. Employers are rarely impressed by the name of a referee who is obviously a friend in a position of responsibility in another company, or a friend of the family.

Other questions asked

Other items which appear periodically on application forms include:

- *previous applications to the same company*
- *names of individuals you know who are currently working for the company*
- *details of current driving licence (and whether you have any endorsements)*
- *languages (with degree of proficiency)*
- *where you saw the advertisement*
- *membership of professional bodies and/or trade unions*
- *countries you have visited and travelled to*
- *details of previous convictions, with dates*
- *notice periods*
- *possible starting dates*
- *dates on which you would be unable to attend an interview*

There may also be a requirement to give details of your aspirations and ambitions. Treat this with care. You must ensure that whatever you say fits in with the pattern for that employer and that you avoid suggesting that you are applying for this post to fill in time or as a stepping stone to something else. If you can find out how long the previous incumbent was in the job, so much the better (if you telephoned for an application form, you could have asked then).

The blank space

Application forms frequently devote a large space (sometimes the whole back page) to a section asking an open question such as 'why are you interested in this job?', 'why do you think your qualifications, experience and personal qualities make you a suitable candidate for this post?', 'why do you think you are qualified for this position?' or simply 'add any details relevant to your application which have not already been mentioned'.

The employer's objective in asking these questions is to make you *think*. You should treat it in exactly the same way as you would formulate a covering letter. Look at the information you have given and bring special points together cohesively so that the sum total of the material makes you seem the ideal candidate. This takes time and you should consider it carefully. If you are filling in the application form just prior to entering an interview, this may give an indication of the sort of questions which will be asked. These questions are typical of those which you should have considered before an interview but can catch the applicant off-guard.

The blank space section can take the form of a career summary, or an overview of the relevant parts of your employment history and personal qualities, if space permits.

Make sure you do not waffle. Everything you say must be relevant to the application. If the form asks you to continue on a separate sheet if necessary, look at the space allotted. If you already have a whole page, do not be tempted to do this – one side should be quite sufficient for this purpose. Continuing beyond this will mean that you lose the impact and are not keeping to a few, well made points.

If you are able to add anything in this section which has not been covered elsewhere, so much the better. There may be skills you have acquired which you no longer use but that are relevant. Similarly, you may be applying to an international company whose parent organisation is in a country where you grew up. Factors like these can be relevant additions, although they would not gain you the position on their own.

Office use only

Most application forms have a blank section which says 'For office use only'. Be careful that you do not encroach on this area – it will be used by an interviewer to make comments about your interview and apparent aptitude for the post.

Photographs

If the application asks for a photograph, it is important to send a recent one. It should be passport sized obtained from a photograph booth if possible. Interviewers can be upset if they expect you to look a lot younger than you do because your photograph was taken so long ago. Also, ensure that it looks like you. If you have changed your hair style and altered your appearance, have another photo taken.

Checklist

1. *Have you photocopied the application form?*
2. *Have you used black ink to complete it?*
3. *Have you studied the job description and any company literature provided?*
4. *Have you filled in the personal information? Is your date of birth correct?*
5. *Have you included the title of the post and reference number?*
6. *Have you put in details of your qualifications?*
7. *Have you given a description of past employment duties angled to the application?*
8. *Have you put in salary information? How close is your present salary to that in the post you have applied for?*
9. *Are your reasons for leaving accurate? What will the employer think of them?*
10. *Are the details of your health accurate and positive?*
11. *Do your leisure interests reflect well on you?*
12. *Have you put in the names and addresses of referees? Have you asked them if they will write references for you? Will the references be good?*
13. *Have you filled in the supplementary information correctly?*
14. *Have you filled in the blank space in such a way that it will be a credit to you?*
15. *Have you complied with all instructions for the application?*

11. Letters of confirmation

There are three main types of letters of confirmation: those confirming the discussion and details to be followed up after interview, those asking about rejection and those confirming acceptance of an offer of employment. All these letters, though simple, need meticulous care and attention. Mistakes here can cost you the job.

After interview

The follow up letter is written to confirm that you are still interested in the position. It need not be detailed or lengthy.

You should thank the employer for interviewing you (without crawling!), but remember that you only need write at all if there is something to say. If you have been set a task, or asked for further information, ensure that you have done exactly as you were asked. If you are unable to enclose the supplementary information immediately, say politely that you will send this on as soon as possible. Do not delay with this and make sure that you do send it as soon as it is available.

If there is nothing further to follow up but you want to contact the employer to prove that you are still interested, you may legitimately contact them to let them know of a change of address, or that you will be away on holiday at a certain time. This will give the impression that you want to be efficient. If you go on holiday but do not tell them, and just expect to reply to any mail when you return, this is not encouraging to the employer as it means an unnecessary delay.

If there is really nothing that you can usefully say to the interviewer, but you are determined to write, make sure that you keep the letter very brief and do not give the impression that you require an immediate answer. The company will have enough to do responding to applicants and conducting interviews without each interviewee generating extra work by writing in. Just say that you enjoyed meeting them, were impressed with the organisation and are still very interested in the position. Do not write saying that you assume they will offer it to you shortly, as this sounds presumptuous.

After rejection

Be very careful when writing to an employer to find out why they have rejected you. You may consider telephoning instead, as the individual within the company may be able to give you fuller details if they do not have to be committed to writing. However, many interviewers are very embarrassed when they receive telephone calls from disappointed candidates, often because they do not really know why they are calling and what they expect to gain from this.

The object of contacting the interviewer in the company that has just rejected you is to find out why, and turn your next job application into success. Never threaten the interviewer. Do not say that you will sue them or that their decision was obviously discriminatory. If you really believe that you were discriminated against, take legal advice from ACAS (the Advisory, Conciliation and Arbitration Service) before contacting the employer again.

Never write to the interviewer's boss to complain or intimate that the interviewer obviously had a bad day! Do not assume that there were no other candidates better than you. You will be unable to change the decision of the employer so do not try. Your aim now must be to look for helpful pointers for the future. You can only do that if you are polite, non-threatening and flatter the employer by requesting some help for the future.

When you compose your letter or plan your telephone call, the points you are aiming to put across must come in the right order to avoid antagonising the recipient. Thank them for interviewing you, making some kind of positive comment about either the organisation or the interviewer (eg. you can say how kind it was of them to be so friendly and for putting you at ease after a difficult journey, etc).

Then you must convince the recipient that you know their decision is final. Comment that you realise that the post was very attractive and that you know that the competition for it was bound to be tough. Then go on to say that you would really appreciate their help though, because this is the kind of thing that you definitely want to do in the future. Ask their advice, say that you are determined to find this sort of work but would very much appreciate advice from the inside. Say that any comments about improving your interview technique would be useful and that if they feel able to tell you why the successful candidate was better you would be very grateful. The object of putting your points across in this way is to lower the defences of the recruiter and seek his or her help. Psychologically you are more likely to enlist their support with flattery, saying that you value their opinions, but do not forget that this can have real value. If you really want to be successful next time, you must listen to the comments that are made for your benefit.

By demonstrating that you do not intend to challenge the decision of the employer you are showing a professional attitude. There is also an outside chance that the person to whom the position was offered will not accept, and your letter or telephone call will demonstrate the fact that you are serious. You will appear to be a reasonable person who respects the opinions and views of the interviewer. If the successful applicant then decides not to accept the post, it may be offered to you.

The other reason for being polite and not challenging the decision of the recruiter, or writing to his or her boss, is that the person may change company and become employed in a similar field. You may find that when you apply there, you do not even get past the first hurdle because the recruiter will remember you as someone who was rude and caused unnecessary trouble at the last organisation. If this kind of coincidence sounds far-fetched, note that it does happen, particularly within similar industries. A past record like this can considerably reduce your employment chances later on.

When you hear from the employer, make notes on the things that you are told and modify either your application or interview style in accordance with the advice proffered.

Success letters and confirmation of employment

Congratulations! You have been offered the post. You must now check the details of the letter offering you the job to ensure that everything is as you had agreed at the interview. If you are unclear about anything, check it. Once you have started the job it is too late to clarify and amend your contract. If you query any points before you start the job you will be in a much stronger bargaining position too.

Some letters offering employment are formal and give all the information that you will need to know. Others seem friendlier but do not give all the relevant details. If that is the case, write back to the organisation saying that whilst you would be delighted to accept the post offered, there are a few points that you wish to clarify. Bring out anything that has been promised to you but does not appear in the letter.

You should reply to a letter offering employment immediately. You should not keep the employer waiting because you think you have a better offer coming up. If you are honestly trying to weigh up the relative merits of more than one offer of employment, telephone the organisation to let them know that you must consider the offer carefully, as another offer has been made. Do not sound as if you are putting pressure on them to give you more money (though you may be offered more), but be honest and give the employer an indication of when they can expect your answer.

There are several things that you must confirm before you accept the position, if these have not been made clear. These include the following:

- *starting date*
- *starting salary (and salary range if applicable)*
- *the grade of your job within the company structure*
- *probationary periods*

- *notice periods*
- *the arrangements for salary reviews*
- *whether membership of professional bodies or trade unions is required*
- *whether the offer is subject to satisfactory medical references*
- *whether the offer is subject to references from previous employers*
- *whether the offer is subject to you providing birth or examination certificates*
- *details of company car arrangements*
- *promotion prospects*
- *the exact details of the contract of employment (including holiday entitlement, canteen arrangements, life assurance, pension rights, hours of work, bonus/commission arrangements, sickness payments, redundancy etc)*

You may not need to check all these points, and there will be others included in a full contract of employment such as disciplinary procedures and absence reporting etc.

Arrangements for salary reviews should be specified so that you know whether you will receive a rise on an annual basis, whether you will gain an increase after three or six months, what sort of progression is usual (eg. progression by merit or fixed annual increment etc). Another aspect which can be contentious is promotion prospects. Sometimes applicants think that the interviewer told them that after a certain length of time they would be promoted. This does not always happen if nothing was put in writing. The interviewer may have meant that this was possible but not automatic.

Car user allowances also often cause problems if the exact details are not specified at the outset. Many individuals also understand that they would be given a better car after a certain length of time, but if nothing is in writing, there are no grounds on which to insist.

If the letter quotes a lower salary than you had expected but the interviewer said that he or she was 'sure something could be arranged', you *must* clarify this before you start. Receipt of your first pay packet or salary advice notice is too late to rectify the problem.

If you told the employer that your holiday arrangements are already made and they agreed to honour these, you should also make sure that you confirm this in writing. Do not ignore the point thinking that it will be all right, because it may not. You do not want to start a new job and then find yourself unemployed only a few months later because the company said that you have taken leave without permission.

Good luck in your new job!

Checklist

After the interview:
1. *Do you need to write?*
2. *Have you managed to sound interested but not over-confident?*

After rejection:
1. *Have you thanked the interviewer or said something good about the interview?*
2. *Have you made sure that the recipient realises that you are not challenging the decision?*
3. *Have you sounded positive and asked for help?*
4. *Have you understood the comments made and altered your CV, general approach or interview techniques accordingly?*

On success:
1. *Have you accepted the position offered?*
2. *Have you clarified any points of doubt and checked on any promises that were made to you verbally?*
3. *Do you understand the details in the contract of employment, or set out in the conditions of service?*
4. *Have you ensured that you can provide any certificates, medical details or references, etc?*

12. Further information

Company background

The following directories and guidebooks will give you more information on organisations. You may require company literature too, but you should find these useful starting points. You should be able to locate these in your local library.

The Financial Times and *The Investors Chronicle* are useful starting points for research on company background. *Extel cards* may also be a useful source of reference if they are available in your library. *The Kompass Directory*, published by Kompass Publishers is also useful. This is a register of British industry and commerce and gives addresses, telephone numbers, names of directors, number of employees, share capital, approximate turnover of the company and the nature of the business.

Key British Enterprises (Dun and Bradstreet) is a list of the top 20,000 British registered companies. It gives information on company structure, names of directors, sales and products with indexes by trade, product and geographical location. Similar is *The Times 1000* (Times Books) which lists leading companies in Britain and includes overseas organisations. It shows domestic and export turnover, capital employed, net profits, number of employees and equity capital for each entry.

Who Owns Whom, (Kompass Publishers) as suggested by the name, shows which companies belong to which others and lists parent organisations with their subsidiaries.

For school leavers, *The Job Book* is published by Hobson's Press of Cambridge and may be useful too. This is an annual guide to employment and training for school leavers and college graduates. Similarly, *Graduate Employment and Training*, (Hobson's Press) also an annual guide, shows career opportunities offered by 2500 employers and has a supplement on graduate studies. *The Directory of*

Opportunities for Graduates (VNU Business Publications) is another annual which gives details of graduates required by employers with information on the training provided by them. It is indexed by occupation, business of the employer, degree subject and geographical location.

The Executive Grapevine (Executive Grapevine Publications) publishes a list of executive recruitment consultants as does *Kemps Recruitment and Training Services Handbook* (Kemps Group), which also lists these by county and by specialism.

It may also be worth checking *Private Eye* which often publishes new information about companies. If your chosen employer merits an interest by *Private Eye*, you may want to think twice about joining them!

On career change/after career breaks

If you intend to change career, read all the information you can find on your chosen field of employment. Careers advice can be gained free through your local council or Jobcentre. You should also try to talk to anyone you know who is working in the field already – utilise your contacts! You may want to write to prominent people in your local industry to ask them for advice – do not expect to take up too much of their time though, as they will receive many letters like yours.

There are many good books on returning to work after a career break. *Returners* is published by the National Advisory Centre on Careers for Women. It is described as notes for those returning to employment later in life or considering training for a new career. Although this was compiled in 1975, it still contains many useful points. Also on this line are *Social Networks and Job Information: the Situation of Women who Return to Work* by Judith Chaney – this is a research project funded by the Equal Opportunities Commission and the Social Science Research Council Joint Panel on Equal Opportunities and *Overcoming the Career Break: a Positive Approach* by Carole Truman (who was

Research Associate at the Women at Work Unit of UMIST) which was written for the Manpower Services Commission.

There are also books on career breaks specific to certain industries. For example, the Engineering Council have produced guidance information for female chartered and technician engineers. If you have a professional body or other relevant organisation, it may well be worth contacting them for any up-to-date information.

For executives

Look at the PER journal, *Executive Post* for vacancies. The Professional and Executive Recruitment organisation is funded by the Manpower Services Commission and states that it is Britain's largest executive recruitment consultancy. PER also issues guidelines on the preparation of CV's and application forms.

Selling Yourself in the Management Market by John Courtis, published by Professional Publishing Ltd. is packed with useful tips and information and is presented in a very readable fashion.

After redundancy

Redundancy Counselling for Managers by Giles Burrows, published by the Institute of Personnel Management gives useful information on redundancy counselling practices and lists many outplacement agencies. Also included are some careers advisory organisations. It may be useful to read a copy of this *before* you are made redundant.

For women

Getting There: Job Hunting for Women by Margaret Wallis, published by Kogan Page gives some useful ideas as does *The Graduate Working Woman Casebook* published by Hobson's Press.

Women are traditionally engaged in more part time work than men and the book *Part-Time Work* by Judith Humphries, published by Kogan Page may be very useful. This covers how to find a job, rights and benefits, employment legislation, case studies and opportunities in part time work.

Disabled applicants

There are a number of books on this subject including *Employment of Disabled People* by Mary Thompson, published by Kogan Page. This covers employment legislation, company policies, sources of advice, etc. It has some case studies and includes material on information technology.

On interviews

This book deals only with the written side of applications for jobs. Although there are many useful books on interviews and interview techniques, the readers of this publication should be aware of several good books on how to be interviewed as opposed to the theory of how interviews should be conducted. Among the helpful books are *Facing the Interview: A Guide to Self Preparation and Presentation* by Clive Fletcher, published by Unwin and *How to be Interviewed* by D. Mackenzie Davey and P. McDonnell, published by the British Institute of Management. The Fletcher book is small, readable and informative and the other has a light-hearted, unsophisticated approach with many amusing cartoons in amongst useful points.

If you are particularly interested it may also be valuable to look at a couple of books on selection testing – many of the larger organisations employ these methods of selection to complement the interview.

13. Examples of CV's

The following appendices give some examples of what and what not to do on CV's. The book has dealt with the theory of preparation but has given few examples of actual entries. To help you see how posts can be described succinctly, there is a 'before' and 'after' example of one of the CV's.

In the first example, the original version and the amended version are shown. The amended version takes the same basic information but translates this into a more presentable format and more readable and interesting CV.

These examples cannot cover every eventuality but give an idea of how to present the CV and how to give useful information about different sorts of posts in different ways.

Appendix 1

This shows an example of a badly designed and presented CV. It is too long, has spelling mistakes and is boringly written. In its full length it reached well over 4 pages!

See also the explanatory notes in the preceding section.

```
Name:  CATHERINE ASCOTT

Address:  70 Aragon Rise
          Amberidge
          Devon  EX23 1YY

Date of Birth:  21.3.87

Teacher's reference number: XXC12

Telephone: Exeter 321
---------------------------------------------
EDUCATION:

Primary: St Anthony's Primary School
         Dumfries, Scotland

   Date: September 1966 to June 1973
```

Secondary: Newton Abbott High School
         Newton Abbott

     Date: September 1973 to June 1980

QUALIFICATIONS:

G.C.E. 'O' Levels: taken in June 1978

Subject   Grade

English literature   B

English language   B

Mathermatics   B

French   C

History   C

Latin   B

Geography   B

Art   A

Spoken English   A

G.C.E. 'A' LEVELS: taken in June 1980

Subject   Grade

English   B

Art   E

General Studies   C

TERTIARY:

   Ulster Polytechnic

   Jordanstown, Newtownabbey, Co Antrim
   N Ireland

   Dates: October 1980 to June 1984

Qualifications obtained:

Bachelor of Education in Communication
Studies, with Honours (Second Class/
Second Division)

Subjects:

1 Literature: a study of English and
French literature and poetry

2 Linguistics: a study of language
patterns as a result of environmental
social and educational factors

3 Language: a study of the structure of
language, both verbally and non-
verbally

4 Drama: An approach to using this medium
of communication in education

5 Media studies: a study of current TV
programmes, films and documentaries,
plus a course on using a video camera

6 Educational studies: an analysis of
classroom activities, teaching practice,
curriculum and development studies.

Subsidiary subjects were psychology and
sociology.

Teaching practices: 2 weeks in Ulster Day
School, 6 weeks in Fermanagh High School,
6 weeks in Bush Juniors and 6 weeks at
Belfast Polytechnic

CURRENT:

Teaching posts: Axle Girls School,
Government Lane, Tangeria

Position held: V.S.O. appointed teacher
of English

Dates: August 1984 to June 1986

Subjects taught: English, Art and Sports

Beckon Residential School for Girls,
Beckon, Amberidge, Devon

Position held: Teacher of form five

Dates: September 1986 to now

Subjects taught: English, Art, R.E.,
                Sports

Non-teaching posts:

Outdoor Camping Ltd, Amberidge, Devon

Assistant Leader of a summer camp for a
youth organisation

Dates: June to early September 1982

White Elephants Retail Ltd, Dumfries,
   Scotland.

Sales Assistant

Dates: July and August 1980 (when visiting
   relatives)

LEISURE PURSUITS:

I am a member of a local tennis club and
take part in many tournaments. I am also
a keen cyclist and travel all over the
country during holiday periods. In
addition, I play squash and netball and
have just taken up fencing.

Arts: I like to paint countryside scenes
and am a keen theatre-goer. I have helped
to organise a production of Macbeth in
the Amberidge Amateaur Dramatics Society.

Reference: Paul Castenella, Ulster
Polytechnic, address as above, and Dr K J
Fitzgerald of Ulster Polytechnic.

Appendix 1A

The following CV is an amendment of that in Appendix 1. It has been shortened and the relevant material brought out.

```
                  CATHERINE ASCOTT

70  Aragon Rise, Amberidge, Devon EX23 1YY

          Tel: Exeter (0392) 321

        Date of Birth: 21.3.62 Age: 25

              -----------------
```

Qualifications:

June 1984   B.Ed. in Communication Studies

June 1980   'A' Levels in English, Art and
            General Studies

June 1978   'O' Levels in English Language,
            English Literature, French,
            Mathematics, History, Art,
            Geography, Spoken English

Education:

Oct 80 - June 84   Ulster Polytechnic,
                    Northern Ireland

Sept 73 - June 80   Newton Abbot High School
                    Devon

Sept 66 - June 73   St Anthony's Primary
                    School, Dumfries,
                    Scotland

Employment:

Sept 86 - now   Beckon Residential
        School for Girls,
        Beckon, Devon

        Post held: Teacher

        I have been in this
        post for nearly a year
        now and teach English,
        Art, R.E. and Sports to
        pupils in form five,
        (15 year olds). This
        involves some remedial
        teaching and work with
        handicapped children.
        I also arrange the
        lunch-time Art Club.

Aug 84 - June 86 Axle Girls' School,
        Tangeria

        Post held: VSO appointed
            English teacher

        Unusually, this post
        lasted for two years,
        giving me wide experience
        teaching disadvantaged
        children over a range of
        subject areas. The groups
        were small but there was
        no streaming and pupils
        ranged in age from 9 to 17.

Leisure interests:

I enjoy most sports, but am most interested
in tennis which I play to tournament level
locally. I am also a keen cyclist, but
often stop for breath and to paint
countryside scenes! I visit the theatre
whenever possible and have recently helped
our local amateur dramatic group with a
production of Macbeth.

    FULLER DETAILS CAN BE PROVIDED

This CV has been dramatically shortened but actually gives more information about the person's character and the posts she has held. The original CV had no detail of teaching duties, no indication of the age ranges of her pupils and too much detail of her qualifications. Whilst these are important for a teacher, the proportion of the CV which they occupied previously was too great.

In the original CV, the teacher's reference number was given which was unnecessary but she omitted her telephone STD code. In addition, the date of birth was incorrect, showing her to be only months old – an easy mistake! The whole CV was badly presented. Nothing was aligned correctly, and enormous space was given to her 'O' level subjects with grades, unnecessary once it was established that she was a graduate. Similarly, great detail was given on the subjects covered within the degree syllabus. These would be better discussed at an interview or provided separately. Note too, that 'mathematics' was spelled incorrectly in the first example.

The amended CV shows education and qualifications before employment history. This is standard within the teaching profession. An employer may want to check these before looking at experience if appointing younger teachers. If all the information is presented in a single page, however, it is less important. Note that all the details are given in reverse chronological order too.

The teaching practices have not been listed in the new CV. These would have been an integral part of any Bachelor of Education course.

In the second version Catherine's hobbies are described in order to make her sound human. The original CV contained too long a list of achievements, leaving no time to teach!

No references have been provided but she would expect to use her current employer and an academic referee. No reasons for leaving are given – it is left for the employer to find this out, but changing teaching posts after the first year is not unusual providing the probation has gone well.

Appendix 2

C U R R I C U L U M   V I T A E

Gail Lambert

66 Lane End, Carshalton, Surrey SM3 3HU

01 - 941 8888

Date of Birth: 24.5.60

Marital Status: Single

Career Progression

Nov 85 - Present   Sales Manager
                    Perfect Publishing Ltd

I have developed market awareness and am
responsible for spotting new trends in
advertising. I recently set up a new
'health' feature to bring in more revenue.
I plan all financial estimates and set
targets for sales staff. High targets have
been set, achieved and maintained whilst I
have been in post, with one third higher
turnover than during the last year.

In addition to supervising the sales staff,
I sell advertising space in the colour
section, visit any new clients
interested in advertising, manage the
printing schedule and liaise on all
aspects of print and reproduction of
photographs, etc.

I recruit, train and motivate all staff in
my section (eleven) and am also
responsible for their appraisals and
disciplinary procedure. I also deal with
all customer and credit queries with two
administrative assistants who also help
me in the day to day running of the office.

Oct 80 - April 82   Secretary
                    Philips Industrial Inks

In the main sales office of this company,
I consolidated all the secretarial skills
that I had learned. My work involved
secretarial duties for the sales manager
and his deputy, and covered all aspects
of initiating correspondence as well as
routine typing, booking hotels and
appointments, diary management and
answering telephone queries. I became
quite an expert on inks too!

Education and Qualifications

Oct 79 - June 80

Elsons Secretarial College
Westerham, Kent

   RSA Diploma for Personal Assistants

   Pitmans Shorthand - 80 w.p.m.

   Pitmans Typing - 50 w.p.m.

April 82 - Nov 85   Sales Administrator
                    HSV Publishing Co Ltd

I joined the company as a Sales Executive
for a weekly publication but subsequently
transferred to Sales Administration work.
In addition to selling advertising space
by telephone and personal contact, I
undertook all the production and layout
for my section of the paper, including
liaison with printers.

In this role, I was also responsible for
any accounts queries and for general
office administration.

Oct 70 - June 78

Coventry Girls' School

June 78 2 'A' Levels in English and
            Communication Studies

June 76 5 'O' Levels in English Language,
            English Literature, Mathematics,
            Geography and French.

Interests

I am a keen member of a ladies football
team and also interested in cookery. I
read novels of all descriptions and
particularly enjoy books by William Golding.

This CV puts in employments before qualifications as these are often more important in a sales environment – the number of 'A' levels is immaterial if the individual cannot sell! It is crucial to show ability to achieve sales targets, and in the sales manager job, to show that the staff are well motivated by the manager and that they are also achieving targets set.

The curriculum vitae suggests someone who likes variety – Gail has not limited herself to selling advertising space alone but has also become involved in the financial side and with running the office. These suggest that she is also well organised and probably a good manager.

The section on qualifications and education (no need to separate them here) shows at a glance the number of 'O' and 'A' levels, which is helpful. The 'A' level in communication studies suggests that the fact that Gail is in sales is not a fluke – she has been interested in communications of various kinds for some time.

The interests are not too numerous and show variation. Gail is outgoing in sport, as part of a ladies football team but also has quieter interests. The point she makes earlier in the section on Philips Industrial Inks shows that she also has a sense of humour.

128